Teaching Values in College

➤➤➤➤➤➤➤➤➤➤➤➤➤➤➤➤➤➤❮❮❮❮❮❮❮❮❮❮❮❮❮❮❮

Facilitating Development of Ethical, Moral, and Value Awareness in Students

Richard L. Morrill

➤➤➤-➤➤➤-➤➤➤-➤➤➤-➤➤➤-➤➤➤◄◄◄-◄◄◄-◄◄◄-◄◄◄-◄◄◄-◄◄◄

Foreword by *Edward D. Eddy*

Teaching Values
in College

->>)->>)->>)->>)->>)->>)<<<-<<<-<<<-<<<-<<<-<<<-

Jossey-Bass Publishers
San Francisco • Washington • London • 1980

TEACHING VALUES IN COLLEGE
Facilitating Development of Ethical, Moral,
and Value Awareness in Students
       by Richard L. Morrill

Copyright © 1980 by: Jossey-Bass Inc., Publishers
                        433 California Street
                        San Francisco, California 94104
                                  &
                        Jossey-Bass Limited
                        28 Banner Street
                        London EC1Y 8QE

Library of Congress Cataloging in Publication Data

Morrill, Richard L.
  Teaching values in college.

  Bibliography: p. 158
  Includes index.
  1. Moral education. 2. Education, Higher—Curri-
cula. I. Title.
LC268.M74   378'.014   80-8003
ISBN 0-87589-475-5

Manufactured in the United States of America

JACKET DESIGN BY WILLI BAUM

FIRST EDITION

Code 8031

The Jossey-Bass
Series in Higher Education

➤➤➤-➤➤-➤➤-➤➤-➤➤-➤➤⟨⟨⟨-⟨⟨⟨-⟨⟨⟨-⟨⟨⟨-⟨⟨⟨-⟨⟨⟨-

Foreword

➤➤➤-➤➤➤-➤➤➤-➤➤➤-➤➤➤-➤➤➤ ⫷⫷⫷-⫷⫷⫷-⫷⫷⫷-⫷⫷⫷-⫷⫷⫷-⫷⫷⫷

Richard L. Morrill's comprehensive, yet personal, view of values and value education on the American campus is the beginning of a new perspective on this entire field. This is a good book because it is disturbing. It pricks precious balloons, and it promotes healthy argument. It raises more questions than it answers because, simply viewed, currently there are more questions than answers in this vast field.

The author maintains that moral education today is heard more often than not "as a pious echo rather than a call to action." And the pious echo resounds uncomfortably when it strikes some emerging concepts of what morality and values are really all about. It is not easy for the American college to break from the authoritarian model of a defender of the righteous faith. It has been discomforting to discover that rigid morality is rejected outright in both form and function by "hedonistic"—but, nevertheless, quick-witted and curious—youth. The tender and the untutored are sophisticates of a new mode of approaching values. President Morrill's volume is an attempt to build a bridge from institution to individual.

Morrill does not go beyond the campus to find answers. He blames, in part, the corruption of liberal education. He says that it has become "even self-consciously, a form of preprofessional train-ing" and that currently it is "dispirited and suffers a loss of self-confidence." He point to the learner who "is split between reason and emotion, knowledge and action, cognition and affection" and who separates facts from values.

In what is perhaps the most revealing writing of the entire volume, Morrill draws on his own creative and frustrating experi-ences in educational administration when he observes: "The past decade has produced a parade of new administrative systems and procedures, most of which have made the administration of higher education ever more like the management of any other organiza-tion, whether it happens to be for profit or otherwise. Student and management information systems, planning and budgeting procedures, personnel systems, management by objectives, market-ing systems, organizational and staff development techniques, all define the world of the contemporary college administrator. . . . Once again, values education's best possibilities initially seem thwarted—in this case by the strong administrative momentum of simply keeping the institution running."

It is not difficult to discern why we have come this far. In the golden, post-World War II years, men with eye patches, sur-rounded by books and bottles of expensive scotch, were depicted by the magazine advertisements as "gentlemen of character." We knew what we wanted from the college or university graduate: unflinching integrity, a stiff spine, a kind but firm heart, and a heavy measure of devotion—not love or passion, mind you, just devotion. Ah, yes, and competence, too. Competence in those terms meant confidence, as reflected perhaps in the pious echo of Kipling: "Ours not to reason why, ours but to do or die." And do they did while their alma maters beamed with pride and took the credit.

"Character education" fell from the academic wall and broke into a thousand pieces when the civil-rights and women's movements plus the anti-Vietnam war era dawned with the severe questioning of authority. The glass of scotch was knocked out of hand and replaced by a picket sign, the bemused smile turned into a furious frown, and devotion was no longer enough. From the early sixties until the mid seventies, the philosophers of ethics could talk only to and among themselves. Morrill has attempted to review the talk, summarize the arguments, place them in perspective, and choose among the most promising of the new directions. Curiously, he eludes a question that perhaps only the students will ask: "Can we (the teachers) be good role models if we are not ethical ourselves?" And we hear the not-so-pious echo of the students whispering, "If it's so great, you try it first. If it works, we might well take it up."

At this point, then, we are raising the potentially crippling query regarding the willingness of students to "take it up." One cannot sit in a value vacuum and devise institutional and academic methods. One must begin by understanding the person who becomes, in the outrageous parlance of the day, "the delivery system" for any set of values. Morrill points to goals and beliefs that "fall short of being values unless they are freely chosen and personally appropriated." In this generation, the most difficult step may not be the formulation and articulation but the personal appropriation.

Based on his experience in both private colleges and public universities, in those that rank among the smallest and among the largest, President Morrill concludes that it is not enough to adopt the Trow-Bronowski-Merton approach of the "powerful morality implicit in scholarly method and procedures themselves," which concludes that "a sound education based on sound scholarship is itself moral education." He prefers, instead, to enunciate the "new educational concern with the themes of choice and decision making." Thus he would ask his students to probe, examine, scrutinize, and push—but to emerge with their own answers. This seems to us a sound approach, though not one which will attract "men of character" who do not quite trust what the student may choose.

Indeed, President Morrill poses between the lines some perplexing questions for the church-related college that knows well what it values and fails in its own estimation if it dares to graduate a student who does not take such values to heart and practice. The public university champions freedom, dissent, and, one hopes, integrity. The private church colleges must wrestle with the hidden affirmation that "this truth shall make you free but not free to doubt and discard." Within the expectation, even the demand, to explore, is there also the willingness to accept the consequences? Morrill confesses that "Americans have a long history of expecting much from their institutions of higher education and continue to do so." Have we led America to expect too much? Are our claims too high in relation to results?

President Morrill has written an enormously useful book. It is filled with definitions, critiques, and discussions. It tantalizes the reader to provide the instances and illustrations for the propositions and possibilities. The author is well qualified by virtue of training, experience, and, most importantly, a keen and sympathetic eye to undertake this comprehensive view. It does not answer; it only annoys. And that, in essence, is the principal task, as Morrill sees it, of all values education.

June 1980   EDWARD D. EDDY
                                                        University Provost
                                                Pennsylvania State University

Preface

Teaching Values in College has two basic goals, the first of which is to clarify and interpret the major current developments in higher education in the areas of moral education and the teaching of ethics and values. The problems in terminology, methods, and goals in this area have become acute, and as a result the current interest in moral education often appears a tangled, confusing set of trends. Thus, a large portion of this book describes the major alternatives in the current discussion by providing a "map" of the terrain. This aspect of the study should be of interest to faculty members, administrators, or virtually anyone else who wants to know more about these topics.

These analyses, however, are offered only as a way to illuminate specific developments and possibilities within higher learning, and not as ends in themselves. In addition to this analytical and descriptive effort, I offer a constructive position of my own concerning values education. This position reflects my long-standing intellectual interest in the nature of moral experience, my service as a professor of ethics, and my involvement in academic administration. Perhaps this background explains the effort that I have made to bring together the concerns of educational theory and practice.

After a brief explanation in the first chapter of the re-emergence of moral education, Chapter Two surveys the current literature and discusses the confusing array of related approaches that have appeared recently. In this chapter I try to distinguish alternatives by developing a basic set of categories: (1) values clarification, (2) values inquiry as illustrated by the work of Earl McGrath, (3) moral education and development in the theories of Lawrence Kohlberg, William Perry, Douglas Heath, Arthur Chickering, and others, and (4) normative and applied ethics, with special reference to recent efforts in the teaching of ethics. The various approaches are compared and contrasted, and each of them is assessed in terms of a set of questions that invariably are raised in an academic context. Do they avoid indoctrination? What goals and strategies are involved in specific educational programs? What is the relationship between knowing and doing the right thing?

Since each of the approaches appears to be deficient in one or several respects, Chapter Three examines the special educational possibilities that reside in a certain understanding of values. Values are depicted as standards of action bearing claims—as opposed to subjective preferences. The discussion goes beyond relativism to provide an interpretation that illuminates the role of values in education.

In the next two chapters I move into the realm of educational practice. Chapter Four, "Methods of Values Education," presents the general methods—values analysis, consciousness, and criticism—through which specific curricular emphases can be developed and implemented. The ultimate aim of these methods is to have students internalize basic forms of awareness and appraisal as to the coherence, consistency, adequacy, comprehensiveness, duration, reciprocity, openness, and authenticity of their values and value systems. Pursued in these ways, values education is able to address many issues and questions more adequately than other approaches. It provides a way, for example, to bridge one form of the gap between knowing and doing.

Chapter Five, "Curriculum and Campus Strategies," suggests specific ways to address values in the classroom and throughout the campus. Although values education is not defined by a single subject matter, certain fields and problems are especially appropriate. These are topics that include significant value choices and involve plausible alternatives. Such topics lend themselves to the kind of challenging give-and-take pedagogy that is necessary in values education. This chapter also makes a strong claim that the campus environment provides an essential context for values education. The nature and quality of human relationships on campus define one of the potent contexts for values education. I suggest how the regular rounds of collegiate life and decision making provide opportunities to develop value awareness and commitment in students.

I assess the consequences of all the proposed methods and strategies of values education in the final chapter, which examines the influence of values education on academic values, democratic values, and ultimate values. In each context, relevant basic values are affirmed while, at the same time, the limits of value commitments are analyzed. The capacity to integrate and synthesize educational emphases that usually are fragmented is the special strength of values education. The typical separation between affect and cognition, thought and action, intellect and conscience, and fact and value is overcome through the integrative possibilities that come through a focus on values. Ultimately, one's aims in education depend upon a perspective about the nature of human knowledge and experience itself.

A resource section at the end of the book provides a brief review of contemporary theories of value and values in the social sciences and in philosophy. These two perspectives need to be related more closely, and this can be accomplished through insights drawn from existential phenomenology. The task is to find ways to study human action and conduct that are not reductionistic explanations. In addition, an annotated bibliography reviews current literature.

Because my thoughts have arisen from so many sources and span several different contexts, it would be impossible to thank adequately the many teachers and colleagues who have contributed to this effort. I would be remiss, however, were I not to mention my special gratitude to Edward D. Eddy. During the countless educational and administrative moments we have shared, he always has demonstrated a primary concern for the effect of education on the lives of human beings. This is a lesson which he has taught constantly but unpretentiously. I have done my best to listen. I also wish to indicate here my appreciation to *Soundings* for permission to reprint several pages from my article "A Conceptual Basis for Values Education in the University" that was featured in the Winter 1978 issue.

Winston-Salem, North Carolina   Richard L. Morrill
June 1980

Contents

➤➤➤➤➤➤➤➤➤➤➤➤ ◄◄◄◄◄◄◄◄◄◄◄◄

The Author

-⟫-⟫-⟫-⟫-⟫-⟫⟪-⟪-⟪-⟪-⟪-⟪-

RICHARD L. MORRILL is president of Salem Academy and Salem College, Winston-Salem, North Carolina. Founded by the Moravians in 1772, Salem is America's oldest educational institution for women in continuing existence still in its original location.

Morrill was awarded the A.B. degree in history from Brown University (1961) *magna cum laude*, the B.D. degree in religious thought from Yale University (1964), and the Ph.D. degree in religion from Duke University (1968), where he was awarded the James B. Duke Fellowship. While an undergraduate he studied for a year in Paris, primarily at L'Institut d'Etudes Politiques. A member of Phi Beta Kappa, Morrill received a Woodrow Wilson Fellowship in 1961–62.

Before becoming president of Salem in August of 1979,

Morrill served as the chief staff officer to the provost of Pennsylvania State University. Prior to that he was associate provost, assistant to the president and associate professor of philosophy and religion at Chatham College in Pittsburgh, Pennsylvania. Morrill began his teaching career at Wells College in Aurora, New York; his primary teaching and research interests have been in contemporary religious thought and ethics.

He is the author or coauthor of a number of articles and reviews dealing with topics in philosophy, religion, and higher education. His articles and reviews have appeared in *Liberal Education, Soundings, The Philosophy Forum,* the *Bulletin of the American Association of University Professors,* and *Foundation News.*

Morrill and his wife, Martha, and their two daughters, Kirsten and Amy, live in the historical restoration of Old Salem in Winston-Salem.

To Martha Morrill

Teaching Values
in College

➤➤➤➤➤➤➤➤➤➤➤➤ ⤆⤆⤆⤆⤆⤆⤆⤆⤆⤆⤆⤆

Facilitating Development
of Ethical, Moral, and Value
Awareness in Students

※»-»»-»» *One* «-«-«

Reemergence of Moral Education

-»»-»»-»»-»»-»»-»»«-«-«-«-«-«

The mission of American colleges and universities has been
strongly shaped by a historical commitment to moral education.
This special attention to moral education has emerged from a variety of sources and has appeared in countless forms and under
many names. It was inspired by the venerable inheritance of Greek
philosophy, informed by the wisdom of European thinkers and
practitioners, guided by the model of the British schools and colleges, and implemented in the characteristic American spirit of
moral activism. Moreover, the intense moral seriousness of the
Jewish and Christian religious traditions has been centrally influential in adding depth to the aims of American higher education. For
a variety of reasons, the religious motivation for moral education
often has been cast in institutional forms. The religious imprint is
evident in the establishment and continued support of many col-

1

leges and universities under denominational auspices. But even when the religious impulse has been absent, as in the initiation and expansion of public higher education, the moral aims of education have been given a prominent place. The practice of democracy itself requires citizens who are not only knowledgeable but also responsible and honorable in the exercise of their freedom. The education of the civic self is a universal theme in American higher education, from the exhortations of the Puritans to the works of John Dewey.

What we loosely have called moral education has assumed many shapes. From the earliest times, it has included study of the Bible and theology as a means of teaching authoritative moral truths. During the nineteenth century especially, it took the form of moral philosophy, with the goal of discovering the oneness of moral truth amidst the variety of human knowledge (Sloan, 1980). Time and again, the broad enterprise has included the provision of formal instruction in ethics as a reflective guide to moral choice. Liberal education, always in theory and often in practice, has focused on moral education and development as one of its essential aims even in its most secular and emancipated forms. The advocates of liberal education propose as educational goals the development of values and civic responsibility through the education of the "whole person." In all these endeavors in moral education, the link between knowledge and action, between intellect and character, always has been presumed to be strong. Throughout our history, we have shown a striking confidence in the power of education—especially when accompanied by a disciplined and regulated collegiate life—to affect and elevate conduct.

The tradition of moral education continues to have a voice, but typically a small one, in most contemporary colleges and universities. More often than not, it is heard as a pious echo rather than as a call to action. It is preached boldly on the commencement platform, but not in the classroom. Although there are obvious exceptions, the major trends in higher education in recent decades have diminished dramatically the force and relevance, the purposes and the plausibility, of moral education. The reasons for this abatement are well known and need only to be mentioned. The autonomy and professionalization of the disciplines, the increasing hegemony and prestige of value-free scientific methodology as a model for all inquiry, and the secularization and pluralism of both our society and the university have established a new educational context. This is a strange and foreign world for moral education. In the academic community, there is little confidence about what can be known in the moral realm, and even less about why, how, and to whom it should be taught.

Recently, there have appeared a striking number of countersignals. The perennial rhetoric about the moral purposes of education has intensified. More importantly, though, it has now been joined by serious scholarship and action, the latter in the form of new educational programs addressed to the broad domain of moral education. As we shall be at pains to point out later, the current interest is many-sided and does not constitute a single movement. Several different languages, each with various dialects, are in use, including discourse about values, ethics, and moral education and development. Although there is a confusion of tongues, there is also a widespread and lively interest in these developments. Countless conferences, articles, books, studies, institutes, and new academic courses and programs attest to the range of the new directions.

Since so many factors in contemporary academic life and thought seem inimical to an interest in values, ethics, and moral education, it is worthwhile to try to explain, if only briefly, the genesis of the current developments. By knowing more about the motives behind these trends, we should be able to assess more accurately their potential and durability. Are we witnessing yet another passing educational fashion, or are there substantial issues that deserve attention and require resolution? We can best begin to answer this question if we situate these new interests within contemporary higher education and society.

The turbulence that marked American campuses during the late 1960s and early 1970s helped both to generate and to mask a serious plea for reform in liberal education. The emerging critique brought to the surface an often inarticulate cry by students for "relevance," which soon was muffled by dramatic confrontations on and off the campus. The more thoughtful critics, however, were raising deeper questions about the evolving nature of the higher

learning and of the academic disciplines themselves. Liberal education, even in small colleges, increasingly was under the dominance
of highly defined disciplines whose subject matter and methods
had become steadily more specialized. The disciplines were evolving into second-order endeavors, increasingly preoccupied with
their own logic, language, and literature. For example, sociologists
were becoming more interested in sociology than in society, and
philosophers were devoting more attention toward proper philosophical analysis than to the nature of truth or reality. Humanists
and scientists were becoming ever more removed from any direct
relationship with questions of value and matters of immediate human significance. This progressive fragmentation of knowledge
stands in sharp contrast with the professed goals of liberal education. Ultimately, each discipline tends to postulate its own versions
of reality by asserting that its method is the only authorized tool
with which truth can be grasped. This assertion sharply contradicts
the purported concerns of liberal education: the student's discovery of meaning, coherence, and purpose among the facts and the
fostering of the student's development as a person.

The meaning of the students' confused cry for relevance
during the late sixties was transformed in the mid seventies when
relevance suddenly came to mean direct preparation for a job.
Liberal education experienced a mounting crisis of spirit as student
enrollment and interest plummeted in the social sciences and especially in the humanities. Students who did enroll in these fields
often did so because professional schools required or recommended a significant amount of work in basic disciplines. Thus
liberal education became, even self-consciously, a form of preprofessional training.

It is no wonder that liberal education has become dispirited
and suffers a loss of self-confidence. By all external measures, it has
declined in importance, prestige, and support, and its sense of
self-worth has been shaken. The internal resources to respond
have been lacking too. Most of the fields in the humanities and the
social sciences have themselves undergone their own professionalization and disciplinary narrowing, far removed from contact with
the dilemmas of human experience and silent about critical questions of personal and social choice.

The current interest in values and moral education is surely related to the disarray in liberal education. The reintroduction of values holds out the promise of a way to integrate the scattered bits of disciplinary knowledge, and offers, moreover, a perspective through which to link knowing and doing.

The turn to values, ethics, and moral development has been prompted by other developments in American life. Ours is an era of critical issues and tough choices. We are surrounded by difficult and intractable problems in American and international society: economic instability and rapid inflation, environmental protection, declining energy sources, world hunger, poverty, racial conflict, population growth, crime amidst affluence, rapid technological change, nuclear armaments, and war and violence. This litany of issues could be extended indefinitely, and in itself may seem merely to suggest the stuff of which history is made. Yet the circumstances we face have a new dimension of seriousness, and our future is fragile and clouded because of it. Declining resources have challenged the bedrock American assumption and imagery of regular, continuing growth and progress. Without recourse to growth as a way to solve social and economic problems, we face a future that requires of us novel patterns of thought and imagination, unfamiliar images of self and society, and new kinds of dreams and visions. They require, too, new forms of education.

We have sensed repeatedly that our inherited values and ethics do not prepare us to address confidently the issues that technology has presented to us. Nuclear power, atomic weaponry, the extension of life through biomedical mechanics, fertilization that occurs in a test tube, genetic engineering—all these recent technological achievements have outraced our ability to decide on their moral consequences for human life. These issues confront our society, but our ethical tradition offers us no ready answers. The result is moral uncertainty and confusion.

These social and technological developments compel us to ask sharp questions regarding the nature and goals of higher learning. Can higher education prepare students to cope effectively and sensitively with the demands of life in tomorrow's democratic society? The debate over technological advances poses conflicts that require difficult and delicate decisions. In a context such as this, value judgments and ethical choices are not philosophical pastimes. They have moved to the center stage of public policy and professional and personal life. Simply enough, the issue is whether colleges and universities can develop the methods to enable students and society to evaluate moral questions effectively and rigorously; or, whether, on the contrary, value questions will be consigned to the realm of emotion and preference, and hence outside the proper sphere of higher learning. The Hastings Center's recent study of the teaching of ethics in undergraduate and professional education reflects these and related concerns (see Callahan and Bok, 1980a).

A series of other reasons account for the prominent place of values and ethics among the present concerns in higher education. Many of them relate to the moral quality of our common life. The apparently perennial feeling that the present is always the worst of times and the past the best, that we are now all drowning in decadence, should never be wholly discounted in explaining high tides of moral criticism. Yet, we are witnessing such provocative and continuing examples of contemporary moral confusion and distortion, that this abiding pattern of woe is only a weak comfort. Watergate is a sobering reality, but also a symbol of deception, broken faith, and distorted loyalties. The common good and public trust were pushed dully aside in the name of tribal pride and self-protection. The trauma of Vietnam provided some extreme examples of these trends in moral consciousness. As William Calley said in his explanation of the My Lai massacre (Sack, 1970, p. 116) "Even if the people say, 'Go wipe out South America,' the Army will do it. No question about it. Majority rules . . . and if a majority tells me . . . 'Lieutenant, go and kill one thousand enemies,' . . . I'll do as I'm told to. I won't revolt. I'll put the will of America above my conscience always. I'm an American citizen." Similar, though far less dramatic, patterns of parochial thought and action have appeared repeatedly in mindless bureaucratic and governmental abuses of personal freedoms and civil liberties, in business bribes and narrow commercialism, and in callous, shoddy, and self-seeking conduct by professionals in all walks of life.

Colleges and universities are themselves subject to a similar moral critique. Students often fail to receive from their institutions even the minimal respect owed to a faceless consumer. Faculty members and administrators face uncertainly a wide array of moral issues in research on human subjects, relations with outside sponsors, admissions and personnel practices (especially with regard to women and minorities), and relations with—and expectations of— colleagues and students. Professional, personal, and institutional self-interest often appear to be the prevailing motivations in all these contexts. Students themselves recently have come to show a striking moral passivity in their attitude toward cheating and campus theft (Carnegie Council, 1979). A minimal morality, or immorality, of privatism and self-protection has eroded the norms and responsibilities of community. These trends prompt us to ask the question, How are students' values affected by their participation in the academic community?

Americans have always expected much of their institutions of higher education and we continue to do so. Faced with signs of moral disorder and uncertainty, our society has a strong expectation that educational institutions should shoulder much of the responsibility. They should both acknowledge their present failures and find ways to improve the moral tone of the nation. Colleges and universities have, after all, always claimed a special capacity to influence conduct and to develop moral character. They are, moreover, the only source of trained practitioners in every professional field. It seems plausible to many, then, to assume that education should address not only the issue of moral reflection but that of moral conduct as well.

It may be helpful to summarize the principal motivations for the current turn toward values, moral education, and ethics. Many contemporary educators and scholars hope that a renewed emphasis on moral education will achieve the following goals: (1) introduce normative inquiry into higher learning, in order to supplement the typically narrow and value-free methodology of contemporary academic disciplines; (2) revitalize liberal education, especially the humanities, and restore the integrative focus that has been lost; (3) provide students with an effective and rigorous preparation for dealing adequately with critical human choices, especially those that have moral consequences; (4) provide an education that affects both conduct and thought, the formation of character as well as the development of intellect.

In our view, the wide interest in values, ethics, and moral

education is best explained in terms of these broader educational and social factors. In other words, in pursuing the best and most responsible contemporary approaches to higher learning, one logically turns toward the sphere of normative choice and its "sciences." Having situated the issue in this way, we now can analyze the diverse forms in which normative inquiry and education are appearing in American colleges and universities. Our review of some aspects of the wider educational issues has provided us with a few tools and measuring rods with which to evaluate the confusing array of possibilities that we shall meet.

➤➤➤➤➤ *Two* ⫷⫷⫷⫷⫷

Approaches to Moral Development and Ethical Awareness

➤➤➤➤➤➤➤⫷⫷⫷⫷⫷⫷⫷

It is worth some effort to clarify the various methods that recently have emerged in the teaching of ethics, values, and moral education. The task is not easy. As in any trend of this kind, the early phases seem to encourage easy agreement and a common language. One can refer broadly to the need for programs in ethics and values, and be understood and affirmed by the like-minded. Yet as assumptions are discussed and actual programs are established, the apparent unity begins to dissolve. One quickly finds that teaching values and ethics and fostering moral development encompass vastly different, even conflicting endeavors. Language tends to hide the diversity as educators use the same terms in decidedly different ways. Serious and deep confusion then typically sets in, as one method or theory is tacitly or consciously assumed to be the whole of moral and values education. So, for example, Kohlberg's theories of moral development, or values clarification, or applied ethics, or professional ethics, or some other approach is accepted by some as the definition of what it means to teach values and ethics. When this occurs, the time has come to classify and analyze the major alternatives that are being proposed.

The differentiae for a classification system could include pedagogical techniques, distinctions between liberal and professional education, or discriminations between applied and theoretical, or between cognitive and affective approaches. We are persuaded, however, that the most illuminating classification is that based on an analysis of educational objectives and their related theoretical assumptions. We shall define four basic categories by exploring what each given approach aims to achieve in the teaching of values and ethics, and from what theoretical or empirical ground these goals are derived. Is the goal, for instance, to teach moral argumentation, to strengthen character and improve conduct, to raise consciousness, or some combination of all of these? We shall probe, too, the level and type of discourse that is involved in the various approaches. Important distinctions among methods result from the degrees of specificity and ambition in their proponents' definitions of values education and ethics. Some are concerned with specific moral acts and issues, others with general principles of conduct or the nature and possibility of normative inquiry itself. The meaning of terms like *values, morals, ethics,* and *moral development* also has to be assessed, for various educators attribute different meanings to these terms. Finally, we shall give some attention to questions of educational strategy and method, especially when these help to clarify goals.

Our effort at classification probably is better characterized as a metaphorical map rather than a formal typology. The goals and assumptions advanced by the different positions are by no means similar enough to be depicted as different versions of the same phenomenon or as part of the same movement. In terms of our mapping effort, though, we can draw an outer boundary that delimits a minimal unity. That common boundary, and the forces that have shaped it, have been sketched in the preceding chapter. The approaches seem to share the pivotal conviction that education must focus on the form and content of human choice. While the commitment to knowledge is by no means abandoned, they shift our attention toward the quality and the consequences of human decisions and actions. Effective methods of normative inquiry and education are needed, their proponents argue, to balance the recent trends of the disciplines, and to contribute to the common good. Broadly speaking, moral education and the study of ethics and values are seen as ways to improve the quality and sensitivity of choice and conduct in several basic spheres of life. Education should address the learner as a citizen in a democracy, as a responsible professional, as a person seeking integrity and fulfillment—and not only as an intellect seeking truth.

Within these boundaries, though, the terrain changes rapidly and the map reveals wide variations. We propose to chart these variations in moral education through establishing and exploring four broad regions: (1) values clarification, (2) values inquiry, (3) moral education and moral development, and (4) normative and applied ethics. In each of these basic categories, we shall examine several specific proposals regarding the theory and practice of ethics and of moral and values education.

Our immediate aim in this chapter will not be to provide an extensive critical study of each option, but to analyze and to clarify their objectives, assumptions, and methods. We need first to get our bearings in a confused landscape. In pursuing this task, though, we will also assess the basic issues, problems, and possibilities facing colleges and universities in the teaching of values and ethics. Our aim is to sketch a broad theoretical and practical agenda to be addressed in the latter half of this book. Our analysis comprises a review of the highlights of the relevant recent literature in American higher education. In the course of our review, we shall pose, often implicitly, a series of fundamental and overlapping questions, ones which inevitably seem to arise whenever instruction in ethics and values is discussed in an academic setting.

1. How do the proposals to teach values, ethics, and morality square with the prevailing academic temper of neutrality in

values and the institutional commitment to serve as a forum for all ideas and values? In a pluralistic society, whose values and which morality and ethics are to be taught?

2. What specific subjects and pedagogical aims and strategies are involved in teaching values, morality, and ethics? Are these acceptable and realistic possibilities for most colleges and universities and their faculties?

3. What is the relationship between knowledge and action in moral and values education? Are there ways to bridge the well-established gap between knowing and doing the good? Can education really affect such things as values? Can and should the study of ethics make one in any sense a better person?

4. What does the basic terminology of a given approach signify? What assumptions do the various alternatives harbor regarding the nature of education, knowledge, and human experience? How do these premises shape an understanding of the purposes and means of ethics, moral education, and values education?

These are the questions we propose to answer after turning to the immediate task of map making.

Values Clarification

The phrase *values clarification* refers to a method of self-discovery by means of which a person identifies or clarifies his or her personal values and value rankings. Values clarification has developed a roughly consistent set of materials, techniques, objectives, and assumptions. Shared understandings and practices stand behind this category, unlike most of the others that we shall study. The basic aim of values clarification is to enhance personal growth through heightened self-awareness. The special educational significance of an awareness of values, especially one's own, comes to light as we explore more fully the presuppositions on which values clarification is based.

Louis Raths, inspired in particular by the thought of John Dewey, has provided the philosophical underpinning of values clarification. He has centered his attention on the valuing process, on the way people arrive at their values, rather than on the content of the values that are chosen. Raths and the most influential theorists and practitioners of values clarification—such as Merrill Hamin, Sidney Simon, Leland W. Howe, Howard Kirschenbaum, and Brian Hall—stress that to hold a value involves an active process of choosing and prizing one's beliefs and behavior and acting on one's beliefs. They describe seven criteria of the valuing process (Raths, Harmon, and Simon, 1966; Simon, Howe, and Kirschenbaum, 1972):

Prizing one's beliefs and behaviors
1. prizing and cherishing
2. publicly affirming, when appropriate
Choosing one's beliefs and behaviors
3. choosing from alternatives
4. choosing after consideration of consequences
5. choosing freely
Acting on one's beliefs
6. acting
7. acting with a pattern, consistency, and repetition

By using these criteria, one can distinguish between values and other forms of human experience and behavior. If one has beliefs or attitudes that are contradicted in action, or if the actions fit no pattern, or if one's choices are the result of external pressures, or if one is unwilling to affirm these choices publicly, then the criteria of the valuing process have not been met. If one's actions, beliefs, and behavior do not fulfill the seven criteria, one's alleged value may actually be something else, such as a belief, an ideal, an interest, an attitude, or a feeling. A person, for example, may give lip service to the ideal of honesty while contradicting it constantly in practice. Through the clarification of his values, that person would learn to see how truthfulness actually figures in his life and what would have to occur for it to become a genuine value for him. Young people, as a further illustration, often voice ideas and pursue goals that they feel will please their parents, but which they have not truly chosen for themselves. All such goals and beliefs fall short of being values unless they are freely chosen and personally appropriated.

We can explore these assumptions and objectives by examining some of the pedagogical techniques used in values clarification. These have become highly visible and widespread in recent years, especially in elementary and secondary education. Their use in higher and adult education, especially in various forms of counseling, is also increasingly common.

Through questionnaires, games, discussions, interviews, role playing, and other exercises, students are assisted in becoming conscious of their values and value hierarchies. In values clarification exercises, an individual might be asked to indicate the amount of time spent on activities such as work, sports, hobbies, travel, and so forth during a typical day or week, or to rank favorite pursuits and interests, or to take a position on a controversial issue, or to imagine various features of an ideal world. Simon, Howe, and Kirschenbaum's *Values Clarification* (1972) is a handbook that outlines seventy-nine specific classroom strategies in values clarification. Brian Hall's *Value Clarification as Learning Process* (1973) is a set of workbooks containing values clarification exercises. Other sources and materials abound.

Many values clarification exercises address one or two aspects of the valuing process, while other strategies deal with all seven. Simon, Howe, and Kirschenbaum (1972) describe a simple classroom procedure, called the Proud Whip, that tests the extent to which students are proud of (prize and cherish) their beliefs and actions. The teacher asks the students what things they are proud of and moves quickly (whips) around the room calling on students to speak. Possible questions might include: What have you done in your school work that you are proud of? What have you made by yourself that you are proud of? What things are you proud of about your family? Tell about a time that you are proud of when you used money wisely. What accomplishments are you proud of in sports?

By using a values grid, students can assess their stances on a given issue in terms of all seven of the criteria of valuing (Simon, Howe, and Kirschenbaum, 1972). An issue can be anything that calls for a decision involving a point of view. It might relate to public issues, personal ethics, professional goals, or whatever. The student records a few words indicating his stance on the matter in the "positions" column of the grid. The numbers from one to seven correspond to the steps in the valuing process. They are to be checked if one's position fulfills the relevant criterion of valuing. That is, is the position something that one (1) prizes and cherishes, (2) has publicly affirmed, (3) has chosen from among alternatives, and so forth, through all seven steps.

Issue	Positions	1	2	3	4	5	6	7

These two exercises illustrate several basic patterns in the procedures of values clarification. In nearly all the strategies, a person begins by citing specific preferences, interests, beliefs, and feelings about such things as family, work, achievements, money, possessions, friendships, controversial issues, and so forth. The next step is typically for the person to try to become fully aware of the value choices and rankings revealed in his or her responses. The general aim is to test the seven value indicators—the feelings and beliefs, attitudes, interests, and concerns about specific objects, issues, and activities—to see if they qualify as values. Another aspect of the procedure is to trace the indicators back to the values of which they are an expression. One's interest in money might point to the underlying value of status or power or pleasure. Strong feelings about unfair treatment of minorities might arise from a commitment to the values of human equality and justice. And so it goes, as the students move to and fro between beliefs and behaviors and the value patterns into which they fit, or fail to fit.

This movement is more systematic and conceptual in some values clarification materials than in others. In fact, many values clarification exercises tend to elicit rather trivial opinions, feelings, tastes, and personal anxieties without requiring the student to devote any significant effort to discovering the value pattern in which they belong. Students end up with only a loose inventory of personal habits and personality traits. Some of the exercises in *Values Clarification* clearly fall into this category.

As has already been noted, one of the important characteristics of values clarification is that in emphasizing valuing as a process, it includes no specific content. It can help a young person or adult discover how to value, but not what to value. The self-awareness it fosters could easily lead to a person's resolving a value conflict, or altering his or her priorities. But such activity depends entirely on the choice and best judgment of the individual. In fact, the exponents of values clarification assert the necessity for neutrality in values with such consistency and force that they are frequently and roundly criticized as thoroughgoing relativists. (For such criticism, see Delattre and Bennett, 1979; Stewart, 1975.)

Some irony usually inheres in any neutral, content-free position that is presented with great moral conviction. This would seem to be the case with values clarification. A close reading of the standard texts reveals, in fact, an interesting structure of basic value content. This becomes especially clear in the significant shift that occurs when the adoption of the valuing process itself becomes a normative educational objective. A move is made from *is* to *ought,* from indicating what the valuing process *is* to asserting that the steps of the process *ought* to be internalized by students (Raths, Harmon, and Simon, 1966). As the total context of *Values Clarification* makes abundantly clear, by following the rules of genuine valuing—choosing and prizing one's beliefs and behavior, and acting on one's beliefs—a person can and should develop a sense of identity, can and should gain control over his or her life, and thereby give it direction. Students can and should become conscious of their choices and affirm themselves, and all this should occur in "a classroom atmosphere of openness, honesty, acceptance and respect" (Simon, Howe, and Kirschenbaum, 1972, p. 21). These objectives clearly depend on an underlying normative structure in which self-affirmation, autonomy, trust, free choice, tolerance, and authenticity are basic values. We have no particular quarrel here with the appropriateness of these values or the normative image of the human person from which they arise. What is lacking, however, is the rationale by means of which these major items of content are derived from what is always presented as a neutral valuing process. Values clarification does not seem to have found the language to distinguish among levels, forms, and types of values nor to articulate its own normative presuppositions. It fails to note how moral values carry very different sorts of claims than, say, personal or esthetic values: "We may be authoritative in those areas that deal with truth and falsity. In areas involving aspirations, purposes, attitudes, interests, beliefs, and so on, we may raise questions, but we cannot 'lay down the law' about what a child's values should be. By definition and by social right, then, values are personal things" (Simon, Howe, and Kirschenbaum, 1972, p. 25). It is rather extraordinary and revealing that truth is not classed as a value here, and that it apparently does not involve aspirations, purposes, beliefs, and the rest. The statement appears to assert two different points: free choice is a test of genuine personal valuing and there is no moral difference in whatever values are chosen. A necessary condition of valuing (free choice) has been stretched into a sufficient definition. It is not surprising that critics seize on this as a sure sign of absolute relativism. The basic problem, though, is a theoretical thinness and confusion that does not enable values clarification to locate and defend its own assumptions.

This brief review makes it clear that values clarification does not understand or present itself consistently as a form of moral education. The overriding concern is with personal values and the personal appropriation of values. The method emphasizes the psychology of personal choice and growth, which it confounds with the nature of values themselves. The obligatory and normative dimensions of the experience of values are given virtually no direct attention, nor does the technique address as ends in themselves the values that inhere in the social and political dimensions of life. Values clarification arose as a way to overcome the boredom and apathy that exist in most classrooms by relating teaching and learning to personal experience. It does not function well as a theory outside of this and similar contexts. When examined as a systematic theory of values, values clarification is unable to answer the questions posed to it; or, it unknowingly provides answers to the wrong questions.

With its present form and emphases, it is unlikely that values clarification will ever play a central role in the academic programs and classrooms of higher education. Most academicians would interpret it primarily as a psychological technique deficient in academic content that best belongs in the career planning or counseling offices. Those faculty members who are interested in ethics, values, and moral education are likely to judge it harshly as overly and unnecessarily relativistic.

Although we are persuaded that these assessments are basically accurate, we also see them as somewhat unfortunate. As a pedagogical technique, values clarification seeks to illustrate the personal meaning of choices and issues. This is a goal that can hardly be dismissed in college classrooms, and one which good teaching always pursues. With some important adjustments, especially in the direction of social and political analysis, the methods of values clarification could enliven many dreary seminars and discussion sessions (see Lockwood, 1978). It could also serve as a device to encourage and yield self-knowledge, an ancient educational objective with perennial force and relevance.

We also see values clarification as offering an important, if partial and flawed, interpretation of the nature of values. This perspective tends to become blurred in the short-sighted insistence that values clarification makes no judgment about the content of value choices. Raths' analysis actually portrays values as a "privileged" form of human experience. They reach the self's very identity, where thought and action are more nearly one, and where the rift between the cognitive and the affective is healed. The long-sought goal of grasping intellectually the unity of personal experience as lived could perhaps be realized through an approach based on values. This is a suggestive possibility, but one not seized or developed in values clarification.

Values Inquiry

Values inquiry involves a broad and basic form of study long in general use in higher learning, but one that recently has become more sharply focused and self-conscious. The term *values inquiry* does not refer to the kind of standardized and definable set of educational objectives and procedures that we found in values clarification. The former phrase is a construct. Although the two are practically indistinguishable as phrases, they represent different approaches with contrasting origins and goals. The two should not be confused, although they clearly are related. The aim of values inquiry is to explore the meaning and possibilities of a human situation by discovering in it the values that motivate human choice and decision. One of the primary assumptions underlying the study of values is the notion that people orient and justify their choices through an implicit appeal to a set of values. To reveal, describe, and assess values is, then, to plumb important depths of the human experience. Since values serve as standards of human choice and embody the question of worth, an analysis of values can disclose decisive aspects of human meaning.

Values inquiry figures prominently in many current proposals for moral and values education (see Donnellan and Ebben, 1978; "The Teaching of Ethics . . . ," 1977). It can serve as a useful way to diagnose an ethical dilemma, to uncover the competing values in a controversial policy question, or to clarify alternative versions of "the good life." Values inquiry and analysis is a descriptive intellectual method, which by no means abandons factual analysis. It seeks, rather, to disclose the qualitative and moral dimensions of human life that may be buried in facts.

We can look to the important work of Earl J. McGrath for a specific set of proposals concerning the possibilities of teaching values in higher education. His writings have been widely influential, especially among small liberal arts colleges, and serve well as a model to introduce many of the issues in values inquiry and analysis. McGrath's interest in values education emerges from a thorough critique of contemporary liberal and general education. He argues vigorously that today's specialized disciplines "produce facts that are of no consequence in the lives of ordinary human beings" (1974, p. 6). Much of the problem, he claims, stems from the dominance of scientism over the whole academic enterprise. McGrath, with many others, contends that the methodology of the natural sciences has been inappropriately applied to the study of humankind. The result has been a model of knowledge and of education in which facts have been radically separated from values and in which neutrality in values has become a controlling norm. In their professional training, most teachers and scholars have learned well the lesson that values are not their proper concern.

As a result, most colleges and universities offer educations that are morally impoverished. The duty of education to develop students' moral sensitivity and judgment has all but been abandoned. This has occurred just at a time when humanity's problems have never been greater and its future never more clouded. McGrath feels that the curriculum of higher education largely has ignored the critical social and human problems of war and peace, international order, racial discrimination, civil liberties, world hunger, poverty, crime, and the environment. Each of these issues, and many similar ones, are characterized by deep and significant value conflicts. They all require choice and decisions based not only on facts and knowledge, but on values as well. Liberal and general education have forsaken their responsibilities by not preparing students to exercise wise and sensitive choice, based on a sound system of values: "No human being can really understand the meaning of his own life or the infinitely complex world in which he lives or maintain any sense of order in his personal or social existence without a commitment to . . . a relatively stable set of values" (McGrath, n.d., p. 29).

McGrath specifically proposes that general education be restructured to include interdisciplinary courses focusing on the pressing political, social, racial, economic, and international problems of our time. These courses would bring together scholars from different disciplines, and the rationale for their joint endeavor "would be found not in the internal logic of each subject but rather in the realities of existence in a complex society" (n.d., p. 36). In tangled and complex life situations, the presence of values is fully manifest in the ways that people make and defend their choices. One of the primary aims of these courses would be to assist students to understand and to clarify the values by which the quality of their lives will be determined. Students should develop the capacity to assess the human consequences of various actions, weighing choices in terms of "the things in life we cherish most highly" (p. 35).

We can begin a brief assessment of McGrath's proposals by noting some of the continuities and discontinuities between his ideas and values clarification. In many ways, McGrath is extending the basic ideas of value awareness and clarification to a communal and social level. In fact, *clarify* and *understand* are the most common terms he uses in presenting his position. While values clarification, however, is primarily personal and psychological, McGrath's concept of values inquiry is focused on social and moral issues. Moreover, McGrath clearly shares the assumption made in values clarification that values possess what we have called a privileged status. They reach deeply into human existence and are "the pulsing blood flow of real life. . . . When a human being recognizes that his values are at stake or under attack he comes nearest to grasping the reality and the meaning of existence" (pp. 31–32).

We find that McGrath is far less reluctant than the practitioners of values clarification to suggest that there is a normative dimension to the choice among values. We are, according to McGrath, to make our choices on the basis of the basic human values we cherish, rather than in terms of considerations motivated solely by technology. Yet, as one probes McGrath's writings for a fuller statement of precisely what these basic human values are, little appears. It is apparent that for McGrath they consist of many of the root values of the Judeo-Christian and the American democratic heritage, but we do not find to date a systematic statement of the particular values that education is responsible to develop. Nor, as we shall see, has McGrath paid much attention to the issue of how the study of values yields changes in an individual's personal system of values.

McGrath's position provides a valuable marker on our map, for it helps to locate a number of related positions and developments. Interdisciplinary courses that focus on a given problem are often part of proposals for change in the liberal arts curriculum. Although these proposals often lack the clear and broad rationale offered by McGrath, they are motivated by many of the factors that he isolates. Perhaps the most visible curricular developments that fit McGrath's proposals are recent courses and programs in science, technology, and society. There are many labels for this interdisciplinary field (technology and human values, science and ethics, and science and the humanities) but all the programs share a relatively consistent set of concerns. In his characteristically vivid language,

Henry Adams offered a prophecy over a century ago, the truth of which is attested to by programs in science, technology and human values: "You may think all this nonsense, but I tell you these are great times. Man has mounted science and is now run away with. I firmly believe that before many centuries more, science will be the master of man. The engines he will have invented will be beyond his strength to control. Some day science may have the existence of mankind in its power, and commit suicide by blowing up the world" (Linden, 1977).

Adams here defines the outer limits of the subject matter and the motivation for the study of the relationships between science and society. Less dramatic yet critical issues fall within the bounds that he sets. The profound influence of science and technology on contemporary social, political, and moral experience is reflected in the typical issues that courses and programs consider in this broad interdisciplinary field. These include the moral and social assessment of technological achievements, public policies regarding the support and control of science, the role of human values in a technological world, the influence of technology on changes in values, the relations between science and other disciplines, and specific ethical dilemmas in science and technology. Courses focus on both these broad issues and on specific topics such as energy, the environment, the arms race, bioethics, computer technology, and the history of technology. As an interdisciplinary field, the study of science, technology, and society uses a variety of analytical and empirical forms of inquiry. Yet, the strongest common orientation is toward questions of choice and decision making. What are the limits and possibilities of rational choice? How can the conflicts between social and scientific values be resolved? To what norms and values can society appeal in setting its course with regard to science and technology? Clearly, normative inquiry has a central role in this rapidly growing field. Values inquiry and normative ethics (another location on our map) are involved in the current programs and courses both implicitly and explicitly. Given the scope and nature of the critical problems at hand, it is hard to see how one could do otherwise.

There will be other occasions in our study to examine the possibilities of values inquiry and analysis, such as in professional ethics. At this point, however, it is useful to begin to place values inquiry in perspective. One important question takes the following form: When the study of values is complete, and the values have been fully revealed and exhaustively studied, what then? If one's analysis has depicted a set of competing and conflicting values—as it usually does—is that the final word? Unless one's choice among values is to be arbitrary, one needs to invoke some principle of selection as a way to supplement and complete one's inquiry and analysis. Values inquiry, in other words, seems to lead naturally to values criticism. Writing on courses in ethics and public policy, David E. Price makes a similar point: "An adequate course [in ethics and public policy] . . . should sensitize students to their own value commitments and to those embedded in the ideological and cultural premises they accept and the analytical techniques they employ. It should also force them to consider alternative, competing values, and perspectives. But I am reluctant to leave it at that: students should move beyond the appreciation of complexity to making and justifying some of the hard ethical choices that must, in fact, be made. It is critically important to move beyond 'laying values out on the table' to precise ethical argument and analysis." (1977, p. 5).

Another important question about values inquiry arises when we consider the relationship between knowledge and conduct. To what extent does a full and clear analysis of values affect the development of a student's own values and the exercise of choice? McGrath, for example, clearly seems to assume that a fuller exploration and understanding of the values domain will itself produce a commitment to sound values. Those who offer or support courses in science, technology, and values are typically motivated by the belief that such studies can make a practical difference. Yet they seem to have given little or no explicit attention to the question of how the transition from knowing to doing will occur. What seem to be missing are first, a fuller account of the criteria for performing an adequate analysis of values as an intellectual task, and second, an explanation of how this analysis can have an apparently decisive effect on human conduct. We do not doubt that there is a potent link between values and action. What we need, however, is a fuller discussion of how and why this connection arises, together with a full presentation of the educational possibilities it offers. In sum, values inquiry appears to be but one step in a wider process of values education.

Moral Education and Development

One of the prominent features on our map is a broad territory called moral education and development. We shall find in it a range of quite different theories and objectives, though all of them center in some way on the concept of human development. Some theorists use the term *development* to include a systematic theory of hierarchical stages of cognitive moral growth, while for others the idea refers straightforwardly to the formation of certain human capacities, relationships, and skills. These approaches are united by a perspective that sets education and moral matters in the context of a broad process of human growth and maturation. Education is seen as contributing to the process of human development by fostering an orientation to moral reflection and choice, a pattern or way of dealing with moral and intellectual questions. There is, however, little or no emphasis in any of the positions on the mastery of a specific moral or ethical subject matter or methodology as intrinsic to moral development. Development may be retarded or accelerated by educational programs, but the knowledge of specific ethical truths does not create, nor is it equivalent to, moral maturity.

Lawrence Kohlberg and the Stages of Cognitve Moral Development. For more than two decades, Lawrence Kohlberg and other researchers have been advancing a theory of moral development and education. Kohlberg contends that education can contribute significantly to cognitive moral growth while avoiding indoctrination. The approach recommended by Kohlberg is based on the view that there are definite stages in the cognitive moral development of young people and adults, just as there are in intellectual and physical maturation.

Kohlberg's work has been deeply informed by the thought of John Dewey and Jean Piaget. He has in particular appropriated and refined their concept of cognitive development. This perspective on cognitive development is of fundamental importance to

Kohlberg's entire enterprise: "Cognitions are assumed to be structures, internally organized wholes or systems of internal relations. These structures are *rules* for the processing of information or the connecting of events" (Kohlberg and Mayer, 1971, p. 457). Cognitive growth occurs not through an automatic and internal process of unfolding, but by virtue of the continuing interaction between the self and other persons and things—the world at large. This process of development involves important structural changes and the reorganization of a child's or a person's patterns of thought. Kohlberg, following Piaget, sees these transformations in terms of a theory of developmental stages. He hypothesizes that the stages involve qualitatively different modes of thought, and that these stages of thought form an invariant sequence that may be speeded up or slowed down but not changed in order. These sequential ways of thinking are "structural wholes," or organized patterns of thought. Cognitive stages form a hierarchy, with each succeeding stage increasingly differentiated and integrated in performing the same function.

Based on this general theory of cognitive development, Kohlberg has identified three moral levels: the preconventional, the conventional, and the postconventional. Each of these levels are divided, in turn, into two distinct stages for a total series of six. These levels and stages were initially derived from interviews with young subjects, and have been tested and refined through two decades of longitudinal research by Kohlberg and his associates. Studies also have been conducted in several cultures outside the United States, and research has been carried out using subjects of various ages. These investigations largely have confirmed the original findings. Interview subjects typically are asked to respond to hypothetical, open-ended moral dilemmas, and their responses are interpreted according to a defined set of scoring procedures and protocols.

The best known of Kohlberg's cases, Heinz' dilemma, serves well to illustrate the approach. Heinz' wife is dying of a disease that could possibly be cured by medication that a druggist is willing to sell only at an unfair and exorbitant price. Since Heinz has no way to obtain the needed money, he steals the drug. Should Heinz have stolen the drug or not? A quick summary of Kohlberg's levels and stages can be presented in terms of various responses to Heinz' dilemma. (For a fuller account of these stages, see Kohlberg, 1976).

The first two stages, which compose the preconventional level, are based on forms of moral reasoning that are not yet in accord with social and moral conventions. In this context, *conventional* refers to the agreement among a group of people to establish and enforce their own standards—conventions—of conduct. In stage one, children judge the rightness or wrongness of an act in terms of whether they are rewarded or punished for it; stage two is characterized by a naive egocentric pattern, with judgments based on whether the ego's immediate needs are being satisfied. Young children probably would expect Heinz to be caught by the police and punished for theft, so they would see stealing the drug as wrong. Children at the next stage would be less concerned with the fact of external punishment, but generally would claim taking the drug to be wrong in terms of the personal pain and discomfort that would ensue. Stealing might lead to imprisonment that would remove Heinz from his family and friends, a sacrifice of his immediate interests and pleasures.

At the conventional level, the stages first begin decisively to mirror obligations to other individuals and groups. Stage three can colloquially be called the *good boy* orientation, since the good is identified with gaining approval and praise. Individuals in this category would judge Heinz to be justified in stealing the drug only if his friends and neighbors would praise him for doing so. *Law-and-order* is the comparable name for the fourth stage, in which an individual sees the authority of the social group as establishing duties that are ends in themselves. The obvious response to Heinz' dilemma from people in this stage would be to censure theft of any sort as destructive of the legal order of society.

At the postconventional level, group standards and laws are usually respected and accepted, but in the name of principles and values that transcend them. At stage five, individuals see social and moral laws as the result of a natural contract made among free people, with the social bond interpreted in light of the utilitarian principle of "the greatest good for the greatest number." In the sixth and final stage, moral reasoning is based on universal principles of justice and fairness, as intrinsically grounded in the individual's own conscience. With regard to Heinz, people in these stages would draw a distinction between the legal and moral requirements of the situation. The value of life would be seen as transcending that of property, so theft would be seen as a morally right action. For many individuals in these stages, especially stage six, there would be a sense that a form of civil disobedience is justifiable under special circumstances. This would include the provision that the "thief" should submit himself to judgment by the law. Since thinking at stage five is strongly centered on the requirements of the social contract and law, the conflict between the legal and moral claims in Heinz' situation would be felt as acute. People in this category grasp less easily and clearly the rationale for a justifiable illegal action than people in stage six. According to Kohlberg, stage six is developmentally and morally superior to the preceding ones. It best coincides with the moral universalism of the philosophical stances of Kant and John Rawls, and can be justified in terms of their theories. These perspectives emphasize that there are universal principles of justice and human dignity that can be discovered by reason.

This brief review reveals several essential aspects of Kohlberg's approach to moral development and education. To be in a given stage is to employ a certain *pattern* or *structure* of reasoning about moral choices. The patterns are essentially differentiated by the basic criteria to which they appeal in order to distinguish right from wrong. One determines the stage by asking: In the name of what underlying principle of organization or cognitive authority, in terms of what implicit point of reference or standard of choice, are moral judgments being made? Based on a number of cross-cultural studies, Kohlberg claims that moral development invariably and invariantly follows the succession of stages. Growth from one stage to another is loosely related to age in children. Even moral and cultural reasoning that is widely different in content shows an underlying *structure* and *organization* of thought that is everywhere and always the same. Moral cognition, according to Kohlberg, does not involve knowing or deriving specific ethical rules of conduct; rather, it concerns the *structures* through which reflection and experience in the moral sphere are first processed and organized.

These perspectives on moral development provide the immediate context and rationale for the approach that Kohlberg and others have taken to moral education. The approach is centered on classroom discussions of difficult hypothetical "borderline" cases in ethics, or more recently, on the kind of social and historical issues that arise in classes in social studies (Fenton, 1976). The discussion leader tries to establish a lively and active exchange of ideas in which students are supportively challenged to justify and defend their positions. In the process, students gain experience in the all-important "moral" skill of taking the perspective of others, and of seeing the self from an external point of view. Through various research projects, Kohlberg and his colleagues have concluded that if discussions of moral cases involve an appropriate degree of "disequilibrium" for the student, such discussions can accelerate the movement to the next higher stage of development. Kohlberg asserts that students can understand and be affected only by reasoning that is one stage above their own. Although this next stage represents a more advanced form or pattern of cognitive thought, it interestingly does not occur through the study and mastery of the content of ethical systems, principles, and rules. One does not develop one's powers of moral cognition by learning the specific methodology and logic of ethics. Rather, in Kohlberg's educational method, one sparks or stimulates moral growth through exposing the student to a reflective tension, to what many psychologists call *cognitive dissonance*. For Kohlberg, following Plato and Socrates, this means, "leading [the student] to see things previously invisible to him" (1970, p. 82). Keeping to a Socratic metaphor, education is the midwife of moral development. The fundamental moving force in moral development is the sum of the social, affective, and cognitive nature of the person, living in interaction with the total environment. The right educational approach can at best precipitate the developmental process into higher stages of morality, which are understood to be cognitive patterns.

This is not the place to offer an extended critical analysis of Kohlberg's position, but several comments are in order. In many ways, his ideas are unusually bold and stimulating. The claims that are made for the scope and universality of moral development are not typical of the caution of most academic theorists, especially those in the social sciences. Here is a perspective on humanity that is rare in the modern era. It concludes that there is a universal and normative human structure of moral reason. The explanation is upward, or humanistic, in its emphasis on human uniqueness rather than on biological drives, psychological conditioning, or genetic inheritance. Neither is it typical to find an effort that seeks, as does his, fully to integrate psychological and philosophical perspectives.

Serious questions can and should be raised, however, about the rather thin base on which such dramatic cross-cultural generalizations have been erected. (See, for example, Simpson, 1974.) The research technique of using hypothetical dilemmas exclusively, and the tricky and pivotal issue of the interpretation of elusive, open-ended responses are also subject to question. The classification system seems to force a precision that does not exist in real life. Of equal concern is the way in which the descriptive logic of psychology has been melded with the normative analysis of philosophy. The sense in which higher stages are "better" than lower ones seems to confound these two forms of analysis. It is peculiar, for example, to find a psychological theory of development asserting the superiority of Kantian ethics (essentially stage six) over utilitarian views (stage five). Philosophers spend lifetimes modifying and reinterpreting these same theories without finding philosophical grounds to provide such a hierarchial ranking. In fact, in many philosophical discussions, the contrast between the Kantian and utilitarian positions is often softened, with a number of noted philosophers claiming that a "mixed" theory is most adequate.

Rather than offering a critique, our major aim is to relate Kohlberg's theories to the enterprise of teaching values and ethics in higher education. Although Kohlberg's work has not focused primarily on college students or adults, his ideas are relevant in this context. His position is increasingly visible in higher education, and he claims that most persons, regardless of age, fail to advance to the highest levels of moral reasoning. The majority of adults are said to be at stages three and four, with fewer than 10 percent reaching the two final stages. Consistent stage six reasoning is very rare (Kohlberg, 1975). If we accept the premises of this analysis, then much could be done in higher education to promote moral development. Kohlberg has argued, in fact, that college attendance spurs the appearance of a special transitional stage between stages four and five. On the surface, it appears to be a reversion to the relativism of stage two, but in reality it represents the students' rejection of conventional morality—though they have not yet replaced it with a coherent postconventional view. This transitional phase can, of course, be seen as coinciding with the relativizing influences of the college experience in which a student typically meets a wide array of new and different ideas, values, and life-styles. (See Kohlberg, 1975, and Middleburg, 1977.)

There would appear to be major problems, however, in the direct appropriation of Kohlberg's theories as the basis for moral education programs at the college level. College faculty members would have little explicit moral subject matter and literature to rely on. Kohlberg's effort has been directed largely toward research and analysis concerning the stages of moral development. His attention to moral education has been subsidiary to this central endeavor. The theory and practice of moral education is basically dependent on the approach used in Kohlberg's original research—the discussion of hypothetical dilemmas. There are, of course, ways to focus the discussion on actual ethical or social issues, but the controlling theory of moral development discounts the intrinsic importance of the subject matter. As we have seen, moral education for Kohlberg does not mean that one actually learns to *do* ethics or moral reasoning. In terms of educational practice, we are left with the general idea of conducting discussions on moral issues in such a way that students are personally challenged. This is a sound approach, but it does not guide one very far into matters of college-level curricular content and pedagogical strategy. The fact that Kohlberg's educational approach does not involve a particular moral subject matter or discipline counts against its wide and direct appropriation in higher education.

Nevertheless, there are suggestive possibilities in the general directions that Kohlberg has set, especially in his theory of moral development. Those ideas can contribute importantly to the selection of course objectives and methods. They provide a framework which an instructor would profit from knowing, both to explain student response and to gauge the effectiveness of course materials and readings. Kohlberg's work offers no prescriptions or content for moral education, but a theoretical base that can be used to pedagogical advantage with existing subject matter.

Other dimensions of Kohlberg's position relate to some of the more general questions that we have been pursuing. We meet again the issue of the relationship between moral thought and action. Although Kohlberg has a broad understanding of cognition, he relates moral development and education to patterns and powers of thinking. Higher forms of moral rationality may increase the possibility of elevating moral conduct, but the gap between reason and action still remains. One can think universally but act egocentrically. Or, in a slight variation of the problem, imagine a petty legalist who understands and avoids violating the highest principles of ethical rationality and yet lives a morally mediocre and disengaged life. Surely, too, as many critics have suggested, Kohlberg must reckon more seriously with the countless studies offered by modern biology, psychology, and sociology that describe how drives, pressures, conditioning, and emotional conflicts control human behavior (see Lickona, 1976). In these perspectives, reason and logic seem reduced to the role of passive onlookers, knowing all but doing nothing. Kohlberg's assumptions about human cognition and affect would not seem to afford him persuasive rejoinders to these interpretations.

Kohlberg is, of course, thoroughly aware of these issues and acknowledges that cognitive moral development is only one facet of the creation of human justice. The full flowering of justice depends upon a community that incarnates it as a principle in human relations and actions. Kohlberg and his colleagues have in fact set up *just communities* in several high schools. Within these small units of approximately fifty participants, students are afforded a large measure of self-governance in order to learn an appreciation of democratic procedures and to develop a sense of community (Munson, 1979). At the same time, Kohlberg is not ready to abandon the centrality of moral rationality. He argues that it is a precondition for moral conduct, for one can scarcely choose a good that one does not know. Although drives and feelings are powerful motivators in moral behavior, without moral cognition these affects would be incomprehensible. They can only be recognized, interpreted, and given a meaning through cognitive structures.

Moreover, Kohlberg contends that moral education has properly and primarily to do with cognition, for to what else can education confidently and properly address itself? In these ways, Kohlberg is arguing that rationality has a kind of priority in human experience. It does not follow, however, that the necessary role of reason in giving meaning to experience is sufficient to control a person's conduct, especially when he is involved in a conflict.

We can conclude this brief review of Kohlberg's thought by noting, not surprisingly, that his fundamental assumptions about human knowledge and experience shape his entire enterprise, and especially his estimate of the possibilities of moral education. His distinction between the cognitive and the affective becomes a hardened methodological separation, and this split necessarily enforces a gap between moral cognition and moral action. When Kohlberg argues that cognitive moral development involves changes in conduct, it seems that, if this is really so, the reasons for it stem from facts about human experience which Kohlberg's own position does not explain. It appears that there would have to be a prior unity between thought and feeling, reflection and action, reason and will, such that change in one would mean change in the other. But if and how this unity exists is not accounted for in Kohlberg's theories, and probably cannot be on the basis of his present assumptions.

The Morality of Scholarship. We turn now to consider several perspectives that, particularly in contrast with Kohlberg's theory, portray moral development as a relatively unstructured process. As our chief model we shall examine an engaging perspective offered by Martin Trow. There also will be occasion to look briefly at several other recent accounts that are in striking agreement with the major lines of Trow's argument.

Trow (1976) argues that the practice and discipline of good scholarship itself contributes to the moral development of students. Scholarly work, in whatever field or discipline, upholds a set of general moral requirements. Trow does not advance or advocate a special program in moral education or ethics to influence students' moral development. He joins a number of other modern thinkers such as Jacob Bronowski and Robert Merton in calling attention to the powerful morality implicit in scholarly methods and pro-cedures themselves. The scholar is required to listen honestly and tolerantly to evidence from whatever the source, to entertain alternative points of view and negative evidence, to engage in self-judgment and self-criticism, and to abandon results that gratify the ego but are not true. Effective scholarship, then, depends upon allegiance to moral and intellectual values such as honesty, tolerance, respect, truth, rigor, and fairness. This distinctive set of values creates a moral community that makes it possible for science and scholarship to function and to flourish.

Beyond the methods of scholarly inquiry, Trow cites the potential moral influence of the teacher. One's values typically are affected deeply through relationships with significant others. When teachers embody vividly the values of objectivity, tolerance, openness to criticism, and intellectual curiosity, they can powerfully influence the goals and aspirations of their students. Teachers can serve as models whose qualities inspire emulation.

The main lines of argument offered by Trow also are found in other recent discussions, including the *Missions of the College Curriculum*, issued by the Carnegie Foundation for the Advancement of Teaching (1977). This work includes a discussion of the morality of the academic community, the values that enable colleges and universities to fulfill their own proper responsibilities. However real the difficulty of achieving value consensus in a pluralistic society, a significant moral content is found in the conditions required for the existence of the scholarly community itself: "We believe that . . . the ideals of the academic tradition, particularly those concerned with respect for truth and academic freedom, provide a reasonable basis for an influence worthy of being generated by our nation's colleges" (p. 245). Distinguishing between those who advocate moral neutrality and those who urge moral engagement, Marvin Bressler makes the same basic point: "This display of moral reticence on the part of ethical neutralists conceals their own unacknowledged, and perhaps unrecognized, commitment to a system of values whose claims are as imperious as any. Educators may remain aloof from all other declarations of moral choice, but they may not refuse to honor the ethical structure that sustains scholarship and teaching. If the neutralists were to concede as much, and the activists were to insist on no more, then colleges could hope to build a consensus around values that all could share" (1978, p. 41).

These proposals and analyses, especially Trow's, evidence

their proponents' underlying concern with the idea that moral commitments and values are part of the development of human capacities. This developmental perspective, however, is both far less structured and wider in scope than are Kohlberg's theories. There is no suggestion of invariant sequences and elaborate stages. The emphasis, moreover, is not simply on cognitive patterns, but includes values as standards of human choice and deep commitments of the self. Attention is focused on the academic community's need and capacity to develop what can only be called intellectual and moral virtues. The emphasis has shifted toward the conative, away from the narrowly cognitive. In their analysis of the dispositions and habits of human action, these educators presuppose that there are certain broad human capacities, tendencies, and forms of consciousness related to choice and character that are subject to development and formation through education.

This proposed academic ethic, it should be emphasized, is taught and learned indirectly. It is a presupposition of scholarship, not its aim. Advocates of this approach to moral development do not suggest any special classroom methods or courses in values and ethics; their claim is that a sound education based on sound scholarship is itself a form of moral education. As students discover the moral requisites for the academic endeavor itself, they come upon an implicit ethic that they learn along with the subject matter, whatever the content. There may well be room within higher education for a larger and more active awareness of its special values, but this in itself does not suggest the need for instruction in morality.

Several critical comments are in order concerning this perspective on moral development. Without doubt, this position effectively reveals the ironic truth that "pure" scholarship is an impossibility, that the most disciplined forms of objectivity depend upon personal commitments to basic values. One cannot conclude, however, that the deep presence of these moral and intellectual values in scholarly work somehow guarantees the moral growth of the person as such. Such a result is potential rather than actual. The pursuit of knowledge in most disciplines is easily and typically isolated from the ordinary decisions of life. The virtues that enable scholarly activity do not appear to have a spontaneous or significant affect on the wide and complex realms of personal and social conduct. The academician's search for negative evidence, tolerance, and self-criticism do not seem to transform the scholar's conduct in university politics, in the affairs of government, or in relations with his or her spouse and children.

Why is this, beyond the cussedness of human nature itself? Surely one reason is the broken vision of truth that besets contemporary academic work. The various disciplines and subdisciplines are admirably able to explore systematically one dimension of nature or of human experience. But this power typically brings with it a narrow focus that fragments truth, even to the point of creating a self-contained version of reality with its own methods of inquiry and private language. The moral virtues that flow from these parochial methodologies easily become defensive and self-protective. They press their claims, but only within fixed boundaries. Often enough, they, like all moral virtues, tend toward self-righteousness. They reject in principle the effort to find a connection either with other ways of knowing or with possibilities for action. Further, as students and teachers of the various disciplines, we are usually unaware or uninterested in the moral virtues that underlie our work. We are not skilled or practiced in unearthing them and in eliciting the wider, humane meaning of their presence. They remain splintered and isolated and fail to transform moral choice, personal relationships, and life directions. Although it might be otherwise, liberal and professional education will have to look elsewhere than to the disciplines themselves for a decisive contribution to personal and moral growth. Their dependency on values is real, but hidden and undeveloped.

Forms of Moral and Ethical Development. A vast number of recent studies have attempted to explore the comprehensive influence of college education on students' development. Their authors typically try to evaluate the effect of the entire college environment on the experience of the student. As a rule, the studies have not focused on moral development alone, nor on any specific efforts in moral education. Thus, much of what they have to report is beyond our present concerns. Several researchers, however, have paid close attention to the development of morality and values as one facet of collegiate experience. It will be worthwhile to examine briefly several studies as they bear on the question of moral and ethical development. Although these authors propose no particular educational programs, their studies have wide and immediate implications for moral education.

William Perry's *Forms of Intellectual and Ethical Development in the College Years* (1970) traces the intellectual development of groups of Harvard undergraduates during the 1950s and 1960s. Based on a series of detailed, longitudinal interviews, Perry developed a set of nine positions, or stages, to classify the results of his research. The positions reflect various assumptions that students have about the nature and characteristics of truth, values, and life goals. Movement through the positions is developmental in nature, with the later positions reflecting more mature or integrated perspectives. In effect, Perry is trying to classify the evolving patterns of the ways students come to "see things" as they encounter the vast and confusing market place of ideas, theories, and life-styles that they meet in and outside the college classroom. Much like Kohlberg, and following Piaget, Perry defines a position as a structure through which thought and experience are processed and organized into characteristic patterns.

Students in positions one and two (*dualism*) tend to see things in black and white, with truth as an absolute and with a final authority as its source. In the early middle stages (*multiplicity*, positions three and four), students acknowledge the existence of multiple points of view, which they have difficulty evaluating. These come to be seen as opinions to which everyone has a right, though they are not in the same category as the still prevailing authoritative truth. By the late middle stages (*relativism*, positions five and six), students have come to see truth as relative. Sincerity of opinion becomes the surest test of truth. The merits of alternative points of view and styles of life are seen so clearly that choice among them becomes difficult, although the awareness of the need to choose begins to develop. In the final stages (*pluralistic commitment*, positions seven, eight, and nine), students explore, at first tentatively and then with more confidence, the affirmation of truths and responsibilities as properly their own. They take and defend personal and intellectual positions while remaining aware that they have chosen one of many options. They establish their own identities within a wider pluralistic world (see Perry, 1970, pp. 57–200).

Perry's conclusions about the nature of intellectual and ethical development offer a number of interesting perspectives. His research studies the influence of the total academic environment, not differentiated by academic field, on the student. He significantly concludes that the most important contribution to a student's intellectual and moral development comes not from the curriculum, but from the realization of community, which occurs as the student becomes aware that he or she is part of a group of individuals who share their doubts and hopes in a common quest. Perry, like Trow, cites the significance of faculty members and others who serve as models and confirm students as fellow members of the community: "Like any other sense of community, this one seemed to derive from reciprocal acts of recognition and confirmation (Erikson). The individual may himself derive a sense of community by observing that others are like himself in that their cares and quandries are like his own. His sense of membership is enormously strengthened, however, if in addition he experiences himself as *seen* by others in the same way" (1970, p. 213). Moral development, then, depends not on *what* subject matter is taught, but on the total process of *how* it is communicated.

Other researchers have examined the development of morality and values as one facet of their analysis of personal and intellectual growth during the college years. In *Identity and Education,* Arthur Chickering (1969) provides a synthesis of a wide range of studies of student development. He seeks to assess the effects of the entire college experience, mainly in four-year liberal arts colleges, and measures these using seven vectors of students' development: (1) developing competence, (2) managing of emotions, (3) developing autonomy, (4) establishing identity, (5) freeing interpersonal relationships, (6) developing purpose, and (7) developing integrity.

Each of the vectors involves a characteristic set of trends, issues, and developmental moments. Following Erik Erikson and others, Chickering interprets these within a broad framework of psychosocial development in which the question of identity is the pivotal issue in a person's varied relationships with the wider world. His discussion of the vector of integrity serves to illustrate this general approach as well as his particular view of moral development. He approaches the topic in terms of the issue of values: "The development of integrity . . . involves the development of standards [values] by which one appraises himself and in terms of which self-esteem varies as a consequence of the appraisal. This definition gives a central place not only to the content of values but to the way they are held and to their salience with regard to behavior and self-appraisal" (1969, p. 124).

The latter point is especially important to Chickering and marks off his approach from other studies of values. A change in one's values occurs not simply when one substitutes one value for another, but as well when one's reasons for holding it, or the way one holds it, alter. With this basis, Chickering presents his findings on the development of integrity in terms of the humanizing of values, the personalizing of values, and the development of congruence.

The humanizing of values involves a certain kind of relativizing of values. Codes and rules of conduct that students saw as absolutes come to be viewed as relative to time and circumstance. They do not necessarily abandon the rules, but apply them flexibly according to the ultimate needs and purposes which they are seen to serve. As students experience the humanizing of values, they typically have to face the anxieties and fears of questioning parental authority, at least as an absolute source of truth.

As students personalize their values, they learn what it means to hold values as truly one's own. One's values "are accepted as part of oneself and as what one stands for. They are consciously held and can be articulated" (p. 139). One's values render a person's choices—of a field of study, of friends, of a future profession—uniquely his or her own. The developmental pattern involves testing values received from parents, peers, and the culture to see if they can be personally appropriated. This leads immediately to the issue of congruence and the development of consistency between a person's professed values and actual values. Congruence occurs to the extent that a person interprets, understands, and acts on the basis of his or her chosen values. Erik Erikson describes human integrity in this way: "Although aware of the relativity of all the various life-styles which have given meaning to human striving, the possessor of integrity is ready to defend the dignity of his own life-style against all physical and economic threats. For he knows that an individual life is the accidental coincidence of but one life with but one segment of history; and that for him all human integrity stands or falls with the one style of integrity of which he partakes" (1963, p. 232).

Douglas Heath has produced several studies of the development of college students that are broadly parallel to Chickering's findings. Heath (1968) has developed a comprehensive model of human maturation that he has used to assess the influence of the college years on students and graduates. Like Chickering, Heath is interested in the influence of the full range of the college experience, not just the curriculum; similarly, he is concerned with students' total personality, not just their intellect. Heath's model of development is more extensive than Chickering's since he gives a great deal of attention to cognitive development, a topic Chickering does not treat.

Heath's approach is founded on his notion of maturity—a complex and multidimensional concept that is able to map important facets of human development: "To become a more mature person is to grow intellectually, to form guiding values, to become knowledgeable about oneself, and to develop social, interpersonal skills" (1968, p. 20). Although we are primarily interested in the maturation of values, a brief sketch of Heath's scheme of development is necessary. Heath divides the human self into four sectors: cognition, values, self-concept, and interpersonal relationships. An individual develops in each of these sectors along five dimensions of maturation, moving from "less" to "more" skill, control, competency, effectiveness, ability, and so forth. The five developmental dimensions are (1) symbolization, or the ability to represent experience, (2) allocentrism, or other-centeredness, (3) integration, (4) stability, and (5) autonomy. If we plot the four aspects of the self against the five dimensions of maturing, the result is a grid like that shown in Figure 1.

One of the grid's components suggests the directions in which people move as their values mature. According to Heath, Haverford undergraduates show significant maturation in their values between their freshman and senior years. They typically develop a greater degree of coherence about their priorities and

Figure 1. Schema of Heath's Theory of Maturation.

	Cognition	Values	Self-Concept	Interpersonal Relationships
Becoming able to symbolize experience	Able to evaluate one's own thought	Aware of one's own beliefs	Aware of self, accurate insights, self-analysis	Able to reflect on relationships and to analyze others' actions and feelings
Becoming allocentric (other-centered)	Able to think logically; thoughts are tied to social reality	Aware of others; tolerance and altruism	Able to see self as similar to others and to empathize	Able to care for others, to love, to be intimate
Becoming progressively integrated	Able to systematically solve problems, synthesize, think coherently	Having a workable world view and coherence in value commitments	Having a congruent self-image and a realistic view of self	Able to be open, to be wholly with another, to have reciprocal, mutual, and cooperative relationships
Becoming stable (resistant to disruption by threat)	Able to organize thoughts and to function consistently	Having a clear, sustained commitment to a set of values	Having a stable and certain view of self	Able to have enduring friendships and commitment to a specific person
Becoming autonomous	Able to use information without bias	Having an independent mind and integrity in belief and behavior	Able to view oneself as responsible and not be overly reliant on others' perceptions	Able to have relationships that reflect autonomy, that are nonmanipulative, and that do not sacrifice integrity for "belonging"

Source: Adapted from Knefelkamp, Widick, and Parker, 1978.

philosophies of life (integration), a wider set of interests in social and political questions outside the self (allocentrism), a fuller sense of holding their beliefs and values as distinctly their own (autonomy), a great certainty about their beliefs in areas such as religion (stability), and an enhanced ability to reflect about values and motives (symbolization). Although these developmental trends in values are significant, they do not rank among top eight areas (integration of values was ninth) out of twenty that students in Heath's study cited as most decisively influenced by college attendance. Students felt the primary areas of influence to be in the integration of cognitive skills; the symbolization of the self-concept; the integration, symbolization, and allocentric development of personal relations; and the integration of the self-concept.

One of the most interesting aspects of Heath's findings is that this ranking of the college's effects on undergraduates is importantly different from the one that alumni report a number of years after graduation. The alumni rank the college's effects in this order: (1) stability of self-concept, (2) stability of values, (3) integration of self-concept, (4) integration of values, (5) development of allocentric values, and (6) development of allocentric personal relations. In a recent study of alumni in their thirties, Heath discovered confirmation for this basic pattern. During interviews, a physician said that college had "impressed upon me the worth of doing something right; it really set standards of excellence." A teacher claimed that "the Quaker ideal came through more strongly than I realized . . . It is with me all the time. I don't think the content stayed with me. That's mostly gone. But the values have remained." An army officer felt that college "had a tremendous influence in forming my ethical opinions . . . made me realize the importance of even having an ethical sense." Heath summarizes his study of alumni by saying that "the college's distinctive, most salient, enduring effect was to permanently alter the character, the values, and the motives of many men" (1977, p. 9).

Heath and Chickering clearly place the development of morals and values within a wider vision of human development. For both, in fact, there is something quite artificial in separating the development of integrity and values from the other realms of the human person. Many aspects of intellectual and emotional growth are preconditions for moral choice, and they are indispensible to its effective functioning. By focusing on this aspect of maturity, we have isolated for analysis certain elements of choice that, especially from a developmental perspective, are part of the dynamic of the unity of the self.

Chickering and Heath offer roughly parallel accounts of the elements of the college experience that contribute to maturity and identity. These elements cut across the full range of college programs and relationships such as residence hall life, peer relationships, curriculum, campus ethos, and relationships with the faculty and administration. Both authors note that developmental progress is related to such factors as clear and consistent objectives, high expectations, a sense of community, the opportunity for students to participate in collegiate decisions and classroom discussions, relationships of confidence and intimacy with peers, and challenging, close relationships with faculty and administration. All these elements become embodied, of course, in particular traditions and practices, such as a college's honor code. As Heath notes, it is very sobering for academicians to learn that the most enduring effects of college do not reside in the facts and theories learned in particular courses. These are soon forgotten. His discoveries have, in fact, lead Heath himself to reconsider the objectives of his own courses and to redesign them accordingly.

It is possible, of course, to explore other developmental theories with a behavioral, social learning, or psychoanalytic orientation. These theories, however, tend to emphasize training, conditioning, or unconscious learning and not the intellectual process that is the basis of higher education. Thus, there are few, if any, recent influential studies from these perspectives with immediate relevance for the practice of moral and values education in colleges and universities.

We might, too, consider approaches being discussed in other countries, especially in Great Britain. The work of R. S. Peters and John Wilson is influential in England, though American discussions of college-level moral education have not given significant attention to these authors. Wilson, in particular, offers a holistic description of morality and moral development that displays its intellectual, emotional, and interpersonal factors. His notion of development is a straightforward one; a given human capability or factor effectively contributes to moral thought and conduct. Thus, sensitivity to others, self-control, emotional awareness, factual knowledge, prescriptive thinking, and so forth, are the "comportments" to be developed through education (Wilson, 1974; Wilson, Williams, and Sugarman, 1967).

As we review this section of our map, we can see clearly significant variations in the terrain of moral development, ranging from a primary emphasis on sequential stages of moral thought to various analyses of the growth of the person. Despite the real discontinuities that we have discovered and noted, several important implications for moral and values education emerge from developmental perspectives. Three points, in particular, merit emphasis. First, in all the positions we have examined, the term *education* has been ascribed a wide meaning. Developmental theorists do not regard education as simply an academic mastery of information or the acquisition of specific intellectual skills. In discussing moral development, they survey the entire college experience as the horizon for education: The curriculum embraces the extracurriculum as a full partner. Second, developmental perspectives place little emphasis on the role of the content of knowledge in producing moral growth and maturity. Content is at most a stimulus to moral development, which is a continuing and inclusive pattern of growth that results from the interaction between a person and the world. Some of the most important and enduring consequences of education seem to take place behind the scenes, so to speak. Clearly, to aim for moral development through education involves rethinking the total process of teaching and learning. Third, a person's developmental stage determines his or her inclusive way of seeing or grasping an issue. Efforts at communication based on a different level of development may simply have no reality for their intended audience. Effective teaching would seem to require the decoding of the students' prevailing developmental patterns.

Normative and Applied Ethics

We reach a final broad plain in our efforts to chart the geography of moral and values education. We find there familiar historical landmarks. In fact, one might well ask whether ethics belongs at all on a map that purports to trace contemporary options in moral and values education. Is it not in an ancient and separate atlas of its own? There are good arguments on both sides of this question, for ethics always has had a significant place in philosophy. Yet, there are certain features in the present approach to ethics that make it a worthy site for exploration.

Until recently, the contemporary philosophical study of ethics in England and America has been primarily concerned with either the history of ethics or the nature and justification of ethical discourse. This latter emphasis is often called *metaethics,* for it deals with the logical, epistemological, and semantic issues that stand behind normative judgments, principles, and rules. The discourse of metaethics pays little or no attention to specific acts, issues, or cases—to the question of what ought to be done in a given situation. The concern, rather, is with such matters as the meaning of basic ethical terms like *good, right, responsible,* and so forth; the methods of justification of ethical claims; the objective and subjective aspects of ethical discourse; and the nature of moral, as opposed to nonmoral, claims and arguments. Philosophers have proposed a wide range of theories about ethical language; some class it as the expression of emotion, others assert that it has the logic of imperatives, and still others argue, in one way or another, for its inherent rationality. In sum, metaethics is discourse about ethical discourse. Ethics has been strongly theoretical, advancing a broad perspective, say, on the nature of the relationship between acts and rules, or arguing broadly for a certain method of ethical reflection.

A widespread and persuasive critique holds that however necessary metaethics and theoretical ethics may be, they should not be the exclusive or dominant forms of philosophical ethics. They often have tended to be narrow and arid forms of inquiry, with little capacity to illuminate the growing complexity and pathos of contemporary moral questions. Not surprisingly, the last decade has seen a vigorous growth in one form of what can be called *normative ethics.* This endeavor has involved, in particular, the effort to explore and to justify what ought to be done in a given moral situation. Typically, this endeavor involves close and rigorous analysis of relevant facts and circumstances and the development or application of appropriate principles and rules of moral conduct. This applied form of normative ethics does not necessarily aim to prescribe another person's moral choices, but seeks to provide a clarification, analysis, and critique of the moral arguments and issues at hand.

The shift toward normative and applied ethics has been accompanied by considerable interest in the teaching of ethics in this mode. As one of many possible examples, we can cite the arguments offered by Derek Bok for the teaching of ethics. Bok (1976) stresses that the central aim of courses in ethics should be to develop the students' capacity for moral reasoning. Moral issues can be discussed with as much rigor as most other subjects, and students can be taught to analyze, justify, and criticize moral arguments. Other potential benefits from the study of ethics include an increase in the students' moral awareness and the development of their moral identity. To achieve these aims, Bok emphasizes the need for interdisciplinary courses that focus on specific problems and provide ample opportunities for discussion and the active exchange of moral ideas and arguments.

Another reflection of the current interest in ethics is the Project on the Teaching of Ethics sponsored by the Hastings Center. The Center has attempted to chart recent developments in the teaching of ethics in American colleges and universities, especially in the context of professional education. The final report of the project (Callahan and Bok, 1980a) cites many of the issues that have been outlined in the present account, including the widespread fear that ethics is too "soft" a field to be taught in higher education. It notes that the interest in teaching ethics is growing rapidly in every major professional field. At the same time, characteristic problems have appeared, including the lack of appropriate literature, unclear objectives, and too few faculty members fully qualified to teach rigorous courses in ethics. The Hastings Center's own commitment to the validity and importance of ethics informs a strong recommendation that ethics be taught as a rigorous discipline according to the highest standards of scholarship and teaching. Like Derek Bok, the Hastings report emphasizes the rational and analytical skills involved in ethics and moral reasoning and places these at the heart of the goals of teaching ethics (see Callahan and Bok, 1979, 1980a).

When understood in this context, the objectives of the enterprise of teaching ethics become especially clear. One teaches and learns ethics much as one would any other discipline. A vast body of tradition and literature supports and defines the field. There are characteristic methodologies and forms of analysis, types of reasoning and argumentation. One can learn to think ethically much as one learns to think scientifically: "The object of ethics is to determine true propositions about virtuous conduct in exactly the same way that the object of chemistry is to determine true propositions about the elements" (Sawhill, 1979, p. 27). One can learn to analyze moral concepts, to identify moral issues, to formulate and apply ethical rules and principles, to advance and justify arguments, and to give and criticize reasons. When new ethical problems are arising on all sides, say the proponents of ethics, ethics should be taught and learned as a rational and rigorous discipline. Ethics becomes a rational tool with which to shape humanity's very future. In contrast with many of the other locations on our map, ethics has a particular subject matter and analytical methodology that can be taught and learned directly. One can teach others the specific steps involved in "doing ethics," whereas this is not possible in at all the same way, for example, in the various approaches to moral development that we surveyed.

Although we have outlined some aims in the teaching of ethics, there is no consensus among educators or philosophers about the nature of ethics. A variety of ethical theories have arisen in normative and applied ethics, each with its characteristic assumptions and methods of analysis and argumentation. Contemporary ethical theories include those that derive their premises from utilitarianism, theories of natural law or natural rights, Kantian ethics, or one of many versions of religious ethics. Then, too, normative ethics includes a range of positions about the relationship between rules, principles, and circumstances. Although educators agree that the teaching of ethics involves teaching normative ethical reasoning, there is no agreement on which ethical theories to teach.

This diversity in ethical theory does not appear to destroy the possibility of teaching ethics in a nondoctrinaire fashion. Despite differences between ethical theories and positions, there is a rather wide consensus on both the methodology and, at a certain broad level, on the content of ethical reflection. For example, certain moral requisites for life in a democracy have become thoroughly institutionalized in law and social practice. Few ethicists have difficulty in assuming the validity of the broad principles that safeguard life, property, contracts, promise keeping, and truth telling. With regard to methodology, they agree that ethical reflection involves a set of characteristic rational steps, regardless of one's philosophical orientation. There is, in other words, a logic to ethical thinking that can be taught and learned without indoctrination. Moral reasoning structures and analyzes problems in ways different from straightforward empirical investigations or prudential calculations. Moral reasons, regardless of the perspective in which they are advanced, tend to assume a quality of ultimacy in decision making. They take a kind of priority over other considerations. As contemporary philosophers have generally emphasized, the moral point of view involves no special appeal to a single individual's or group's desires. Moral judgments tend toward generalizability, toward the test that the same rule or same action ought to be adopted by anyone in a similar situation. Even when philosophers propose different theories of morality, they tend to use similar analytical procedures in exploring specific issues.

As we have noted, these methods of moral reasoning now are being pursued widely in applied and professional contexts. Applied ethics, the use of moral reasoning in specific cases and quandries, aims to explore issues and reach decisions regarding specific problems and types of problems. Although applied ethics involves rigorous analytical methods, it is not merely a neat exercise in deductive logic. Far more is involved than the mechanical application of general principles to individual cases. Bioethics, probably the most prominent field in applied ethics, serves well to illustrate this point. In studying bioethics, students typically grapple with ethical dilemmas that arise in areas such as abortion, the care of dying patients, genetic engineering, and the use of scarce medical resources. Students learn, among other things, to analyze ethical issues. Arguments and their implications are elicited, relevant facts are uncovered, and prime concepts and ethical principles are spelled out. Clouser (1976, p. 45) describes some of the issues that confront medical ethicists: "Is abortion killing the fetus or simply removing the pregnancy? Is not treating the same as killing? What results from interpreting it one way or the other? What constitutes being a person? Fetuses, the severely retarded, the senile—are they persons, and do they have certain rights? If yes, then such and such follows; if no, then something else follows. And so on." Even once one has identified all the issues and arguments, one may not be immediately able to make a decision. One may require more factual information or a more detailed analysis of the relevance, consistency, and adequacy of a given argument. In many circumstances, several morally permissible options may appear; in others, no decision seems wholly able to avoid evil consequences. Applied ethics, in sum, uses all the precision and rigor at its command, but its powers are circumscribed by the difficulty and complexity of the real cases with which it must deal.

Bioethics also reveals a special dimension of contemporary normative and applied ethics. Technological advances have created unforeseen and unprecedented issues that require decisions. The framework of inherited ethical wisdom is constantly shattered by new problems arising from scientific, technical, and medical discoveries and inventions. Thus, as one quick and obvious illustration, the traditional categories and rules regarding the taking of human life do not provide an immediate answer to questions about whether physical life should be sustained endlessly through a respirator. The questions of when death occurs and of the type of effort that should be applied to sustain life are not simply provocative academic puzzles. In bioethics and environmental ethics, in the nuclear field and elsewhere, ethical questions are at the heart of an array of legal, social, and policy issues that profoundly influence institutional practice and everyday life. Ethics is thus a practical science that negotiates society's entry into a complex future. In this way, it makes a special and intensely practical contribution to social well-being.

Professional ethics represents another distinctive form in which the current interest in the teaching of ethics has emerged. Nearly all professional fields have begun to give at least some attention to the ways in which professional training can develop professional responsibility. This concern is, without doubt, motivated by the recurrent criticisms of professional self-interest and avarice, and the periodic, glaring examples of individual misdeeds, whether in the media, law, medicine, government, education, or business.

The study of professional ethics involves several different clusters and types of issues. Perhaps most obvious are specific ethical dilemmas that professionals confront in the course of their work. A definite choice is required as to whether, depending on the profession and the circumstances, one will lie to a patient, reveal a serious problem in a government contract, protect one's sources, make public confidential or privileged information, or disobey a superior's orders. In these cases, a decision between several courses of action is required, and ethics functions as a reflective guide to choice. Depending on one's profession or case, one might have to apply and interpret a code of professional conduct, testing the relevance and applicability of a given standard to the case at hand. In the more typical situation, in which there is no detailed code, the individual would have to work through the meaning of a general ethical principle, such as truthfulness, confidentiality, or privacy, for the specific case. One would require all the tools of careful and rigorous ethical analysis to guide one's course of action.

In the effort to develop and to teach a specific code of professional ethics, we find special forms of ethical reasoning that link the general requirements of morality with a particular moral office or social role. Two norms often must be reconciled in codes or concepts of professional responsibility, those of the profession itself and general ethical principles. At one extreme, the norms of the profession are equivalent to a formal etiquette of professional identity and belonging. They are ethics in the descriptive sense that any group, even a band of thieves, has a set of norms through which it defines itself. The ultimate penalty for violating a norm is removal from the group. On the other hand, a professional code must encompass universal ethical principles of justice, respect for life, truthfulness, and so on, principles that apply to all persons. These two sets of norms are merged in professional ethics. The priority of now one, now the other, reveals much of the ethical dynamic and meaning of a particular professional code or set of expectations. Clearly enough, in this context, to learn ethics is to master the code, or the equivalent, that expresses the profession's normative self-understanding, and to learn the forms of moral reasoning that the profession uses to develop these rules and regulations.

It would be a mistake to confine professional ethics to a concern for ethical quandaries and codes. The enterprise is wider than this and includes an interest in the analysis and development of professional responsibility. Professional ethics might well involve the effort to analyze the moral ideals and social responsibilities of the profession's members, the value commitments and conflicts in which they are involved, and the normative pattern of relationships they have with clients and colleagues. Professional life historically has meant a calling to service and social responsibility, a meaning that is easily lost in a bureaucratized and institutionalized society. As these various analytical tasks are carried out as part of professional ethics, it is likely that the definition of the term *ethics* will become blurred. In some cases, the enterprise may seem to fall more clearly into our categories of values inquiry or moral development. The resolution of specific dilemmas and the development and dissemination of an ethical code—ethics in the narrow sense— obviously depend upon a prior analysis of the values and general responsibilities of the profession.

The issue, too, of the individual's own professional integrity is a pivotal one in contemporary professional education. How does an individual learn to translate the mastery of a theoretical code of ethics into responsible professional behavior? Although one might well argue that a concern for moral dilemmas is at the center of the terrain of professional ethics, an accurate map of the actual region cannot neglect the neighboring territory of professional conduct. Surely, the goal of improved conduct has been central to the actual motivation for teaching professional ethics in the first place. How the teaching of ethics can achieve this goal is another question.

We have classified ethics, even in its applied and professional forms, as a discipline. In contrast with values clarification, values inquiry, and moral development, ethics is a specific field of study with characteristic forms of reasoning. To teach ethics is to teach this subject matter and these logical and analytical methods. Because ethics occupies this place on our map, it is relevant to raise certain of our recurrent questions about it.

As the discipline of moral decision making, ethics is clearly not primarily intended to influence directly a person's behavior. If only intellectual and logical skills are stressed in teaching ethics, it is unlikely that these courses will influence the student's moral growth as a person. One could claim that ethics does influence conduct whenever rational analysis provides the right reasons for choosing a given course of action. Precisely as the science of moral choice, ethics always has a potential relation to behavior. This claim assumes, though, that the relation between ethical knowledge and action is unperturbed by other motives and passions. In the face of competing influences on conduct—which is typically the case— one's mastery of ethics does not in itself enable one to act properly. Ethics aids our recognition of the right choice, but cannot empower it. In fact, of all the positions we have surveyed, ethics presents the widest form of the perennial difference between knowing and do- ing the good.

There are other ways, too, in which the teaching of ethics as a discipline presents special problems in the applied and profes- sional fields. As we have defined it, ethics is a field that, like virtu- ally any other, requires a trained professional to teach it. To expect those not trained in the subject to teach it is to endanger the basic quality of education. The proponents of the teaching of ethics, however, often have just this expectation. One simply must realize that few individuals can both teach professional ethics while prac- ticing the relevant profession. Either we must change and widen the definition of ethics or give those with professional expertise or knowledge of ethics special training in the field in which they lack preparation. (For a fuller discussion of the teaching of ethics, see Callahan and Bok, 1980b, chap. 3.)

Conclusion

Having sketched the contours and prominent features of ethics and moral and values education, what final boundaries can we draw on our map? In what ways do the various positions share a common horizon, and how are they situated in unique environs? Further, can we now answer the fundamental questions that we raised at the outset about the limits and possibilities of moral and values education?

As suggested in Chapter One, the current interest in ethics

and in moral and values education is best explained as a development within liberal and professional education. The value choices
and ethical dilemmas facing contemporary society have revealed
the need for new directions in education. The existing form of the
disciplines and the actual goals of higher education have not
proved adequate to the demands of our society.

The various approaches we have suggested do not necessarily accept each element in the moral diagnosis of society or in the
critique of education, nor do they, by any means, present their
emphases in the same way. They do share, however, the opinion
that the phenomenon of choice must be a primary educational
concern. Some educators emphasize the reflective aspects of
choice, others the active dimensions as depicted by theories of
moral development. In every case, however, there is a concern that
education must treat the themes of choice and decision making in
addition to offering students the mastery of a methodology or the
acquisition of information. The center of educational attention is
shifting toward the question, "What ought to be done?"

In the course of our review, we have seen diverse and even
contradictory approaches to an education for effective choice. The
many sources of this diversity include different terminologies and
opposing assumptions about the nature of education, knowledge,
and human experience itself. The different approaches, too, are
directed at varying levels and types of education. Finally, these
proposals represent different ranges of educational effort. Values
inquiry, for instance, could be incorporated in virtually every
aspect of the curriculum, while ethics has a more defined methodology for dealing with specific moral issues. In this sense, ethics would be one particular form of values education. We can
continue to sort out the emphases in the different positions by
returning to our original questions about the appropriateness of
teaching ethics and moral and values education in a pluralistic
academic environment.

The widespread fear that ethics and moral and values edu
cation involve indoctrination or arbitrariness does not seem to be
warranted. In fact, all the positions that we have explored share a
self-conscious concern to avoid moralism or the advocacy of a specific set of ethical conclusions or values. The emphasis in each case

has been either on a *process* of inquiry, a *mode* of reasoning, a *pattern* of development, or a set of *fundamental* values. There is, indeed, a democratic or academic moral point of view buried in many of the recommended educational objectives and procedures, but it is so general that anyone living in our social, political, and educational order must make similar commitments. In fact, many critics of these proposals probably would conclude these educators avoid moralism only because their proposals provide no real moral content, that is, they do not offer guidance as to what one ought to do or how one should live. This criticism, of course, depends largely on prior and tacit expectations about how much moral content is enough. Whatever one's opinion, it is fair to conclude that the relationship between the process and content of moral and values inquiry is a pivotal concern. On this relationship turns the issue whether ethics and moral and values education are appropriately part of the university's responsibility, whether the enterprise has something of real substance to offer. It deserves further consideration.

Our survey did not reveal any highly structured or elaborate curricular programs and pedagogies. We found instead a series of techniques and emphases that have varying degrees of definition and self-consciousness. The most defined and formal methods appear in the study of ethics. Here there is a clear requirement for specialists, at least in many contexts. Many of the other proposals, however, could call upon the actual and potential skills of a wide range of faculty members. Faculty members would need to develop some special techniques and analytical tools. How faculty would acquire these skills is an important and unanswered question.

A variety of other pedagogical continuities and discontinuities in the alternatives are worth signaling. Among a number of the positions, especially in moral development, there is virtually no emphasis on the transmission of information as the primary means of moral education. One does not learn values or morality, it would appear, simply by hearing lectures, reading books, and mastering facts and theories. Moral truths and values are not ready-made pieces of information that can be transmitted from mind to mind. Many of the proposals that we have surveyed advocate a practical or participating method for teaching moral values. We find a repeated emphasis on the need to promote active discussion that will create some disequilibrium in the students' minds. It also appears in the frequent suggestion that students consider real problems that present contrasting perspectives and underlying conflicts of values. Thus we are not surprised to find case studies and case histories as the most commonly used and recommended form of reading material. We also find, however, especially in ethics, an emphasis on disciplined and rigorous moral reasoning that can be learned as one learns any field. In all, we notice a wide and rather disconcerting split of opinion among the various educators as to the importance of studying a specific subject matter.

Our earlier question concerning the relationship of knowledge to action, or of moral theory to practice, seems to fall decidedly short of receiving an adequate answer. Given that values, morality, and ethics have to do precisely with deciding and choosing—with action—this particular relation between knowing and doing, by nature, presses for full connection. Yet, we find only partial answers, avoidance of the issue, or acceptance of the separation. We hear an expression of hope that knowing the good through ethics might lead to doing it, the unsubstantial belief that this will occur through values analysis, and the assumption that the development of certain moral dispositions through education will influence conduct. These views may well have their measure of truth, but we have yet to find a coherent theory of how education succeeds in providing the link between thought and action.

The reasons for the enduring gap are not hard to find. They emerge clearly as we consider the images of human nature and experience that stand behind the various theories. Although it is easy to forget, any systematic and comprehensive theory of education entails a view of human possibilities. Our first question in education should be, What does it mean to be human? One cannot talk about education without positing the subject of the learning. We find that the theories we have examined typically assume a learner who is split between reason and emotion, knowledge and action, cognition and affection, and who lives in a world in which facts are separated from values. The various positions seem unable to forge in theory the links between knowing, feeling, and doing that we live as persons. When we understand more fully what it means for the unified human person—not a mind in a body, or an organism in an environment—to be the subject of education, then the full possibilities of moral and values education will be manifest. In many of the positions that have been surveyed on our map, we have found signposts pointing the direction in which we should travel. Now the task is to begin our journey and explore the educational integration that it demands and promises.

-»»-»»-»» *Three* «-«-«-

Values as Standards
of Action

-»»-»»-»»-»»-»»-»»«-«-«-«-«-«-«-

A map provides a guide to various locations, but it cannot guarantee one's satisfaction with what one finds on arrival. This describes our situation. The various proposals for ethics and moral
and values education resolve some of the educational problems and
questions that surround them, but others remain and continue to
press their claims. Our present aim is to outline an approach that is
adequate to the issues with which values education must contend
and is responsive to the demands of the present and future.

Our chosen point of departure is values, and our ultimate
goal is to describe a coherent and effective approach to values
education. To reach this goal, however, we must relocate the present discussion, moving beyond the assumptions of the existing approaches to find some fresh perspectives on values and on human
experience itself. Most of the proposals we surveyed in Chapter

Two, and the criticisms of them, develop from sharp separations between fact and value, the normative and the descriptive, the cognitive and the affective, form and content, and knowledge and action. Distinctions of this sort are necessary and useful in all analytical work, but they easily and often assume an independent life of their own. When they become reified entities or ideological slogans, we lose all sense of the underlying unity of human experience that the categories originally were meant to clarify and explain. After all, when things go wrong, we do not hold accountable flawed cognition or affect. In real life, we judge the entire person, the responsible human agent who is "in" and yet "behind" all thoughts and actions. One can, of course, try to deny, displace, or explain away the original unity of consciousness. Yet in the moral sphere, it is terribly hard and unpersuasive to do so. And it is impossible to do this in our roles and responsibilities as we actually live them. Our first task, then, is to search for a way of thinking that integrates our distinctions and more directly relates them to our experience as agents. It should allow us to see the deep connection between intellect and conscience, between knowledge and responsibility. Such a perspective is available in a certain understanding of the nature of values.

When approached in the appropriate way, values education offers a broad set of possibilities for an education oriented toward effective and sensitive choice. It meets the tests of a comprehensive educational emphasis on choice and decision making more successfully than the various options we have examined in moral development and ethics. An approach based on the appropriate understanding of values provides the following possibilities: (1) the means to introduce normative inquiry into education in a broad, rigorous, and nonpartisan way, supplementing the specialized methodologies of the disciplines; (2) a way to investigate and illuminate the moral and human consequences of choice; (3) a means to revitalize liberal education, especially the humanities, and restore the integrative focus that has been lost; (4) the ability to address questions of character and conduct in their unity with matters of thought and knowledge.

Pursued in this way, values education would be broader than ethics or moral education, and would include them within it.

Values education, defined by the foregoing educational objectives, would provide the setting for these other enterprises. It would not, therefore, include or endorse just any approach to ethics, but only those that addressed the special concerns of an education for choice. Abstract ethical theory, especially as pursued in the metaethics of the past few decades, would not be of particular interest in values education. Rather, applied and professional ethics, in the forms in which they recently have come to the fore, would comprise part of values education as understood here. Like any other discipline, ethics is intrinsically worthwhile. Yet its present prospects, its rapid growth, and its new importance are to be understood in terms of its ability to meet the requirements of a vital, responsive, and humane form of liberal and professional education.

These strong claims for the general possibilities of values education cannot be taken at face value. They require special justification, for the enterprise is subject to serious questions from a number of directions. "Values. A terrible business. You can at best stammer when you talk about them," is the way Wittgenstein characterized one aspect of the problem. Serious terminological problems exist as scholars and educators use basic terms like *value, values, valuing,* and *value judgments* to connote widely diverse meanings. Many discussions of values in higher education make very little progress precisely because speakers do not clearly define the meanings of their basic terms. We already have seen several aspects of this confusion in our review of values inquiry and values clarification. We hope to avoid this problem by carefully defining our concepts.

As complex and difficult as the question of terminology is in itself, it quickly leads to deeper issues regarding the very nature of human knowledge and experience. Many, perhaps most, contemporary academicians assume that values are subjective in nature and wholly a function of personal choice and desire, that they are preferences. To seek to influence another's preferences is to intrude on personal freedom, to meddle in private matters, and to set arbitrary standards. From this viewpoint, instruction in values lies beyond the proper scope of higher learning. Colleges and universities should limit themselves to their proper business—the discovery and transmission of knowledge and the development of the skills of the intellect. Educators should bear no responsibility for shaping a student's values, for that task can be accomplished only through indoctrination. Since differences in values cannot be resolved by an appeal to objective criteria, the attempt to teach values is alien to the basic purposes and responsibilities of higher education.

The position described here is obviously one expression of the prevailing academic temper of our times, a disposition that can be characterized loosely as the mood of relativism. Since any discussion of values has to contend seriously with relativism, we must now examine its characteristic orientation and assumptions. We are less interested in it as a formal doctrine than as an element in the atmosphere of contemporary rationality.

Relativism

The concept of relativism suggests that there are no enduring and general, no absolute or universal, standards for human conduct. Whatever standards exist are tied to special conditions, relative to particular times, places, and cultures. In the realm of values, and to a large extent this includes even moral values, relativism involves a way of thinking that highlights the uniqueness and appropriateness of individual desires, felt needs, personal circumstances, and contingent social conventions. The resolution of differing viewpoints becomes impossible since no objective, rational standards of validity exist. As William Perry's research has shown, virtually all students find higher education to involve a relativizing process in which unquestioned beliefs of all sorts are debunked. Students pass through phases in which they hold utterly private notions of conscience. The prevalent intellectual atmosphere neither accepts nor supports the principle that an educational institution has responsibility for shaping its students' values.

Although it has many sources, the mood of relativism derives in large part from the dominant definitions of objectivity upon which most modern academic disciplines are based. Most of modern scholarship traces its own progress to the objectivity and neutrality of its value-free methodologies. Students soon learn that the terminus of rationality has been reached, that the discussion can end when someone is able to assert, "That's a value judgment." The special meanings that the terms *value* and *values* have assumed in academic life are captured by the psychologist Robert White in his comment about science and values: "Science has trouble with values. The scientist, setting himself the worthy goal of objectivity, which requires the overcoming of personal idiosyncrasy and preference, came to think of values mainly as sources of error, if not of opposition to the very cause of science" (1964, p. 322).

Most fields, modelling themselves on the natural sciences, have devised powerful explanatory tools that seek to penetrate to the basic causes, forces, and influences behind a given natural, social, or even interpersonal event. These analyses seek to break the event, including human events and moral standards, into ever smaller bits of information. We explain by decomposing the whole into its parts and providing quantifiable evidence to support our claims. The immediacies of factual experience grip our attention, leading to skepticism concerning any claims to discover structures and unities behind particulars. Such analytic explanation often is equivalent to "explaining away." In analyses of this sort, a human activity such as valuing—which takes place precisely through integrating beliefs, feelings, and actions—is difficult to grasp. The specific unified quality of valuing eludes the analyst.

Another factor contributing to the dominant mood of relativism, especially in the educational experience of most students, is the radical shift of perspective as one moves from discipline to discipline. Students are often troubled or amused at the way each field assumes its own centrality and necessity. One never seems to grasp reality, but only that slice of it afforded by the disciplinary instrument at hand. William Perry (1970) has traced the evolution of the use of "multiple frames of reference" in final examination questions in certain courses at Harvard University from 1900 to 1960. In virtually all fields, he notes a steady and marked increase in questions that ask students to compare different views and interpretations (that is, to use multiple frames of reference), rather than simply to give the right answer. Thus, even within a single discipline, the emphasis is typically on analyzing different positions and contrasting alternative interpretations. It is not surprising that many students temporarily or permanently come to see "sincerity of opinion" as the surest measure of truth. Nor is it startling to find that students have trouble seeing the relationship between different methodologies and disciplines. The integration of knowledge seems far too pretentious and impossible a task to receive much attention in most college curriculums. The relativity of different ways of knowing remains an unassailable given in the great majority of contemporary approaches to education.

Important social factors also contribute to the temper of relativism in higher learning. Contemporary colleges and universities reflect the cultural pluralism of the nation at large. Students and faculty members come from a vast array of different cultural, ethnic, and religious traditions. The culturally determined quality of values seems inescapable in a pluralistic context. To many, the teaching of values appears a euphemism for the inculcation of the dominant group's way of life.

This disposition to relativism accounts for much of the diffidence and caution among some educators about the possibility of values education. Yet values education entails other difficulties, too. Even if one were to suppose that values are objective, many would argue that higher education has no effective ways significantly to affect them, at least through the curriculum. Values are the product of strong parental, cultural, and psychological factors and forces. They are not items of knowledge to be learned simply by taking thought. As one common slogan has it, "values are caught, not taught." It would seem best, in light of this, that the university not accept goals it cannot meet, nor set expectations that can only be disappointed. It already has more than enough to accomplish in its proper tasks of discovering and transmitting knowledge.

These general cautions and issues help to set the agenda of our proposal for values education. They add a special dimension to the questions that any proposal for moral education must answer. We need to know what is the appropriate subject matter of values education and to find ways that values can be studied and analyzed. We have to discover as well whether colleges and universities are responsible for values, and how this responsibility can be met. We begin with a brief interpretation of the nature and function of values. (This account is supplemented by a more technical discussion of methodology that appears in Resource A. In Resource B there are suggestions for further reading on value theory and many of the other authors and positions that we have reviewed.) Our expectation surely is not to legislate a final and comprehensive definition of the role of values in human life. Rather, our aim is to develop an understanding of values that is able to illuminate both their actual and potential role in liberal and professional education. Obviously, one's proposal for values education is strictly predicated on one's interpretation of values.

Defining Values

Our discussion of values comprises four fundamental topics: the definition of values, the process of valuing, the objectivity of values, and the relativity of values.

Values can be defined as standards and patterns of choice that guide persons and groups toward satisfaction, fulfillment, and meaning. Many abstract nouns that are subsumed by this definition come readily to mind: honesty, integrity, courage, care, freedom, order, justice, pleasure, compassion, status, loyalty, security, friendship, trust, success, love, efficiency, peace, power, tolerance, respect, and so forth, finally to include several hundred terms in ordinary usage. When these words are used to refer to a person's or a group's values, they allude to relevant normative patterns and standards of choice. Values serve as the authorities in the name of which choices are made and action is taken. These same terms are, of course, often understood and used in several other ways. Some could be classified as emotions, others as concepts, some as attitudes, several as ideals, and most as one or more of these things at various times, depending on the context. Yet, as values, the specific reference of these words is to forms of human agency, to criteria of self-determination. In this definition, in contrast with that offered by values clarification, values are not specific things, beliefs, actions, or value judgments. Such particular things as a sum of money, a work of art, a hobby, a law, a promotion, a nice house, a political office, a loving act or warm feelings are not values. These specific things, actions, and experiences are indicators or expressions of values; they are the desired and desirable realities in which valuing always is embodied. Values are mediated through these particulars, and can be located only by means of them. In themselves, however, they are not values but form part of a larger pattern of value-oriented choice. Values are being depicted here as modes of existing and choosing, as qualifications of human agency.

It will be helpful to explore the implications of our definition by examining again the description of the valuing process that we encountered in our review of values clarification. (See Chapter Two.) It provides helpful insight into some aspects of the distinctive ways values function. Although it clearly needs to be supplemented and corrected in several important ways, it effectively distinguishes values, as valuing, from related forms of experience. We recall that, according to Louis Raths, valuing includes the three basic dimensions of prizing and choosing one's beliefs and behavior, and acting on one's beliefs.

This characterization of the way values actually function in life reveals that the term itself can be misleading. *Values* easily suggests a static and abstract entity akin to ideals or essences. By referring to values in terms of valuing, we are able to focus on the active or verbal aspect of a human process. We are enabled to see that holding a value, that is, valuing, involves an active positioning of the self with regard to its own beliefs, conduct, and feelings. Valuing is a stance or orientation assumed by the self through prizing, choosing, and acting—all in relation to a given situation. This description also reveals a theme to be explored later, that valuing unifies knowing and doing and is integral to both.

We can isolate the distinctive nature of values by comparing them with related phenomena, such as attitudes, feelings, beliefs, ideals, and concepts. This comparison reveals that values include a generic and definitive element of commitment. In this sense, commitment is self-enactment, agency, or action, where this latter term refers to the carrying out of an intended project, including mental or cognitive projects. Values exist precisely as the standards in, of, and for action. If one's standards change, so does the meaning of one's action. If one alters significantly one's actions, so one alters the standards in the name of which they are carried out. For this reason, values are never fully actual except as they orient choice and shape conduct. A purported value that fails to press its claim in relevant action of some kind actually is something else, perhaps a belief, an attitude, a feeling, or an ideal. Friendship, for instance, exists fully as a value only as acts are performed and evaluated in its name. One may have all sorts of beliefs, attitudes, and feelings about friendship that fail to shape one's actual ways of relating to other people. (For further discussion of the differences between attitudes and values, see Rokeach, 1968, chap. 7.) When values are understood as self-involving commitments, an important truth about them emerges. They are seen to be a central and germinal factor in a person's basic identity.

Another important aspect of the valuing process, and one that is often overlooked, concerns the authority of values and the demand or claim that they introduce into human consciousness. One's experience of the claim pressed by a value is closely related to, yet distinct from, the characteristic of prizing one's beliefs and actions. Not only do our values attract us, they also ask things of us and hold sway over our consciousness of ourselves. We experience values as commitments to action which urge us forward and through which we hold ourselves accountable. Values, then, exercise authority by pressing consistent, and often stern, claims and demands. Through values the self calls itself into question and judges its own behavior. Not all values are moral values, by any means. But every value bears an "ought" with its own specific weight that engenders various forms of obligation and self-evaluation. Valuing is indeed an affair of the heart, of prizing and cherishing but, as in all love relations, there are accompanying demands, expectations, duties, and evaluations. Lovers of truth, or freedom, or justice or pleasure, are also servants who know the striving and self-judgment that service entails. (For an extended discussion of the authority of values, see Mehl, 1957.)

An illustration may help to clarify several of the special emphases in the foregoing interpretation of values. Let us consider tolerance and the special features that are brought to light when we interpret it as a value. As a standard of choice, tolerance is a person's immanent principle of selection; it is a personal stance toward the world. To hold tolerance as a value is not to simply entertain it as an interesting abstract concept and adopt an attitude favorable to it. One's values constitute a pattern of motivation and choice, a structure of intention and action. One who values tolerance orders and organizes his or her intellectual and psychological responses to ideas and people in the name of tolerance. Through tolerance as a value, one chooses to listen rather than to turn a deaf ear, to accept others' differences rather than to insist on agreement as a condition for the relationship, to support the right to dissent rather than to seek to banish or destroy the unfamiliar. At each point, one chooses among alternative responses, among contending feelings, thoughts, and deeds. The pleasures of reprisal, the self-assertion of absolutism, the security of rejection—all are psychic and intellectual possibilities that hold their own attractions. One who has adopted tolerance as a value has adopted a structure of choice that favors and prizes acceptance and understanding as a criterion for choice. One's values effect a way of structuring and intending, of ordering and organizing, the full range of emotional, mental, and moral appeals with which the self is constantly and endlessly solicited. This is what it means for tolerance to be a standard of choice, to be a qualification of human agency, to be a value. A person who verbally endorses tolerance, but whose choices and actions are not oriented by it, does not hold tolerance as a value. For that person, tolerance is perhaps an attitude or a belief, but it is not an actual value. One may have good reasons for temporarily or permanently abandoning a value, but that process involves its own justification and careful reckoning. As we have suggested, to value tolerance carries claims and obligations as a dimension of its reality. One does not casually choose to follow or abandon one's actual values, one's structures of intention. Through the experience and actualization of values, something important is at stake in the self's own estimate of itself.

Our definition of values contains an implicit normative dimension. We earlier asserted that values, as standards of choice, lead to satisfaction, fulfillment, and meaning. This definition now leads us to the difficult and important question of whether values are subjective or objective, relative or absolute. We must consider the content and meaning of values and the sense in which they can be said to be objective. Our description of the valuing process needs to be supplemented, and distinctions made between forms of valuing that are truthful as opposed to deceitful, just as opposed to unjust, or creative as opposed to destructive. As we explore the objective dimensions of values, we find it necessary to abstract values from the flux and complexity of ordinary experience. We need to understand values as such, before exploring value choices and conflicts. Perhaps the most serious flaw in values clarification is its failure to discuss values in these fundamental terms.

Let us begin by contrasting abstract nouns that connote values with their opposites—truth and falsehood, justice and injustice, love and hate, honesty and dishonesty. The pivotal distinction between these pairs brings to mind a point that is constantly and easily forgotten because it is so basic—that a value, to merit the term, calls forth thought and conduct that has worth, that leads, at least under the right conditions, to the fulfillment of human potential or to the discovery of a variety of types and levels of meaning. When a value is adopted by an individual, it comes to reside in a pattern of human agency, it becomes a mediator in the complementary relationship between a human life and the world. The notion of complementarity suggests that there are objective characteristics and structural possibilities—not desires and whims—on each side that make the relationship what it is.

Already we can see the two entities that it is the task of values to relate: *self* and *world*. This relationship occurs constantly and unconsciously, day in and day out, both in the humdrum of the ordinary and in the rare moments of brilliance and creativity. Since it usually does occur in forgetfulness, it is important to show what is involved in this unconscious but primordial connection. One way to do this is, in effect, negatively. To attempt to abstract values from this relationship, or to claim that one cannot see them, quickly shows itself as an impossible effort. Such a world would be a formless chaos, a radically unpredictable source of potential that would be unresponsive to man's effort to humanize it; in such a world, any action would be possible at any time, and all actions would be equally impossible and arbitrary (Mehl, 1957).

That human relationships with the world need not be, and are not, at this impossible level is explained by the presence of values. Through values the world becomes a human dwelling place. There is, then, a type of objectivity that is characteristic of values as such. Values are neither arbitrary nor capricious. They are not the creation of desire, whim, or fancy. They provide the standards for the exploration, development, and expression of human possibility. They give us the patterns for the effective initiation and unfolding of the human project in the world. The world (including physical nature, social and cultural forms, and other persons) presents itself as a limit, as an encompassing and cumbersome presence, as a multiplicity of tasks to be performed upon pain of succumbing. It has a being of its own, offering innumerable possibilities both for satisfaction and frustration, creation and destruction, life and death. The task of values is to link human needs and purposes with the opportunities and obstacles of the world. When these two entities have been brought together to the fulfillment of man, value has been actualized. Values give rise to those patterns of choice through which human beings are enabled to solve problems, to avoid impasses and impossible situations, and to create an open future (Mehl, 1957). Values, then, are an expression of the complementarity that can pertain between human conduct and the world. If there is a real world, then values are objective.

The objectivity of values reveals itself in any number of different contexts in human life, but the sphere of interpersonal relations offers a compelling illustration. Values provide the standards through which the individual ego can escape from complete preoccupation with itself, from its own essentially isolated and arbitrary moods, feelings, impulses, and desires. As "natural" beings, human beings are a collection of spontaneous tendencies and individually defined physical and psychological characteristics. A relationship between two individuals founded on this basis alone could only mean differing forms of combat, domination, and exploitation in the name of the immediacies and private desires of one ego against another. Through common allegiance to values, however, an "I" and a "you" can become a "we," tasks and demands can be shared, and the potential isolation of existence can be overcome in a relationship. Through accepting the authority of values, individuals become persons to and for one another. The private factors of individuality—moods, drives, desires, impulses—are shaped and fashioned by the demands inherent in communication and relationship. Understood in this way, values provide human beings with the very possibility of existence as persons. Values, at this fundamental level, clearly are not subjective preferences but the conditions of possibility for meaningful human experience.

One could claim that the values that are constitutive of personal relationships—truth telling, promise keeping, empathy, trust, respect, and the like—are simply social conventions or the products of positive reinforcement. Some existentialist philosophers might argue that such values are valid only if they are freely accepted by a sovereign and transcendent consciousness, which can invent other forms of freedom at will. Yet as one explores the implications of interpreting values as arbitrary, these positions seem quite discordant with primary human reality. Consider a world in which one chose arbitrarily to lie to people, to manipulate them, to treat them as objects, and to break faith with them. The ordering of thought, feeling, and action by truthfulness, respect, and trust would give way to the brute expansion of the ego. Whatever the psychological or the logical status of conduct of this kind, it is clearly impossible and destructive in terms of human possibility and meaning. It constitutes exile from human communion, it entails the impossibility of existence as a person, it leads to total solitude. Whatever kind of existence might be possible if values were arbitrary, it would not be recognizably human. One cannot coherently imagine a human world in which values were merely a function of desire. (Mehl, 1957, discusses the relationship between value and person. The present account is an interpretation and application of his work.)

We have attempted to depict the objectivity of values as such by discussing how they provide the conditions of possibility for the discovery of a meaningful world. Yet much of our experience of values undeniably reveals their relativity. They exist in a mixed form as relational patterns, combining both absolute and relative features. They are relative to the structures of human potential. In addition, the implementation of values in daily life makes their actualization a function of changing circumstances and personal choice. As we have noted, this subjective pole of our experience of values largely has captured the imagination of the modern academician.

The relativity of values shows itself in the enormous and incalculable range of factual conduct that can issue from a value or a set of values. Values orient choice, they do not determine it. The same value can be the source for a myriad of divergent expectations, procedures, and actions in different cultures and different persons, and even within the same person, as circumstances change. The moral value of respect for human life, for instance, is translated into many different rules of conduct. Through this value, we posit that killing is wrong, but we then usually refine that principle into a prohibition of murder. As we analyze the features of certain types of moral situations, we come to the conclusion that killing in self-defense and killing in wartime combat are not murder. These general principles and rules, in turn, are filtered through many shapes and shades of culture and personality, and result in specific empirical behavior. Each culture and person has a set of social, religious, and psychological "rituals" for expressing its special sense of the value of life. Through all these levels of choice, the same value is present as a structure of intention. At some point in the stages of choice, of course, one value may cooperate with another, confront another, or altogether cease to be a value. Is it the value of respect for life or that of technological efficiency that leads one to sustain the life of a severely brain-damaged, terminally-ill patient through artificial means? Even though a value marks a direction and sets real limits, it is best understood as inspiring conduct without determining all the particulars.

The relativity of values is further apparent in the choice among values—in the different rankings that individuals and institutions choose to give to various values. Justice, freedom, equality, love, security, trust, pleasure, success, and countless other values enter into complex relations with one another, and with existing circumstances, to shape the actual content of human life. The decision of which value to favor in a given situation is characterized by enormous diversity and relativity. We refer with great tolerance, for example, to the different life-styles that people adopt and see these as essentially private value choices. We ordinarily neither praise nor blame those who choose urban over pastoral pleasures, or rank the needs of the family higher or lower than other values, or place an ordered life above or below a free and spontaneous one. Max Lerner (1976, pp. 123–124) states well one aspect of this issue, "The bind lies in the still unresolved tension between polar values: to work hard *and* to be casual; to make a living *and* to make a life; to reject materialism *and* to afford travel, technology, and gadgetry; to be free for personal growth *and* to raise children as well; to be open to adventure *and* to be commit-ted to continuing love and family loyalties; to care for country . . . . *and* to be a citizen of the world; to explore new modes of consciousness and awareness *and* to continue embracing the every-day pragmatisms of life." In the choice among values, the doctrine of relativism seems highly persuasive, for the question of which good to choose, and how and when to choose it, is not easily resolved.

The modern conscience is especially sensitive to these con-flicts in the choice between and among values, to the clash between two or more pursuits, each of which on its face is worthy. Economic growth vies with environmental protection, freedom of expression with the right to privacy, international order with national security, compensatory justice with procedural fairness. So common are these conflicts, that our language has developed special terms to express the problem. We speak constantly of *options* and *trade-offs* in order to suggest that virtually every decision involves sacrificing some benefit and accepting some ill effects in the name of the chosen good. Rarely do we think and act in terms of a fixed hierarchy of values that consistently subordinates the lesser to the greater good. Rather than a hierarchy, a plurality of contending values seems to set the stage for our decisions. We quickly lose sight of the shared values that support pluralism because they are so basic. Discord and diversity seem to outweigh consensus. We will return to this theme of the relativity of values in our discussion of values education, remembering that this relativity exists within a wider objectivity, which we can specify and define in ways that are important for education.

Types of Values

Before bringing this rapid survey of the nature of values to a close, we must examine another common confusion. It is often assumed that all values are moral or ethical in nature, that to be concerned with values is to adopt a moral stance. The call to attend to values in higher education usually is made or is heard as a moral appeal. It should not be. There are, in fact, a large number of different types or spheres of values in addition to those in the moral realm; for example, intellectual, esthetic, political, personal, economic, and social values. In each of these areas, values characteristically carry demands and press claims, though in nonmoral ways. Intellectual values such as truth, clarity, consistency, and rigor are often morally neutral. We do not usually view errors or inconsistencies—only deception—as meriting moral blame. Obviously the whole of life is oriented and structured by values, so a concern for values need not be directed to the moral dimension of experience alone.

The source of this tendency to reduce all values to moral ones is not difficult to locate. Moral values typically regulate human conduct at the level of humanity's basic uniqueness, dignity, and worth. They are the guardians of the humane, of the properly human. As a result, they tend to take precedence over other values. Values in other spheres that fail to respect these basic human conditions find themselves in conflict with moral requirements and come under their judgment. Compromise, for instance, is an autonomous political value up to the point that it violates the value of moral integrity. The special surveillance of moral values is also clear even in the sphere of personal values. As persons go about the task of developing a particular way of life, they are faced with the necessity of ranking values and choosing among priorities. As we have seen, these typically are autonomous decisions in which people face a wide latitude of acceptable choices. Yet there is clearly a moral aspect to this choice of the kind of person one becomes, and whether, say, status or integrity, power or love, service or ambition, will become the controlling value. In itself there is, for instance, no moral issue in the decision to relax by taking a stroll. But if that is all one does, especially while being needed elsewhere, one's choice of values enters the moral sphere.

The Priority of Values

It will be worthwhile to pull together several conclusions that emerge from the interpretation that we have offered of the nature and role of values. We have interpreted values as a privileged form of human experience. There is a sense in which they can be seen as "prior" to thought, conduct, and feeling. The priority in question, however, is not chronological, nor does it necessarily involve a ranking in terms of the essential and the unessential. The priority of values resides in their providing the dimension of a situation that makes it a meaningful and possible human situation in the world. Thought, feeling, and conduct are always in the name of values, always structured by values. Thought, feeling, and conduct are always subject to the more original effort of the self to inhabit a meaningful world. The scholar who seeks true propositions is locked into his reflective activity by a demand—truth as a value—that regulates his search and is not exhausted by any of his specific judgments. The reformer pursues social change in the name of justice, coming under the standard it provides, and no individual act exhausts justice as a value. The lover of pleasure searches for and prizes enjoyment, but, through values, prefers some pleasures to others and endlessly conceives of new satisfactions. At no matter what point one penetrates into the life of the self or a culture, one finds a structure of values that enforces claims and standards. Since these values are the qualifications that constitute and inform all efforts of the self to be a self in this world—ultimately, to exist and not succumb—no other forms of consciousness precede valuing. Human life is given as value-charged and value-laden, as already and necessarily conformed to the authority of values. To propose that other forms of consciousness somehow precede valuing would be to suppose that one could climb back to some moment in the life of the self not already subject to value. To claim that either thought or conduct or feeling itself constitutes the basic nature of values is to try to locate values without first having found a unified self to whom to refer them. But neither of these moments can ever be found. One must conclude, therefore, that the existence of values is coincident with the constitution of the self (Mehl, 1957).

This description of the priority of values should not foster the notion that they are somehow separate in time and in personal experience from thinking, doing, and feeling. To forestall this interpretation, we have to recall the given unity of consciousness and the simultaneity of its different forms and dimensions. Although values are not themselves beliefs or judgments, they necessarily come to expression in and through thought. Although values are not feelings or emotions, they inevitably involve desires and fears. Although values cannot be defined as deeds, they always are mediated through specific acts. To paraphrase and expand on Kant: Values without reason would be blind, without feeling would be impotent, and without deeds would be empty. The significant implications of this interpenetration of the forms of consciousness will become apparent in our discussion of values education.

>>>->>>->>> *Four* <<<-<<<-<<<

Methods of
Values Education

>>>->>>->>>->>>->>>->>>)<<<-<<<-<<<-<<<-<<<-<<<-<<<

The interpretation of values presented in Chapter Three serves as a starting point for our approach to values education. Our understanding of values as normative standards and patterns of choice enables us to answer various sets of questions that have been posed about the possibility and goals of moral and values education. From the preliminary conclusions we reached in Chapter Three about values, we can now propose three hypotheses that we will test in our presentation of a framework for values education.

First, values have normative and objective dimensions that are consistent with the university's methods and responsibilities. Any description of its role that omits the aim to foster fundamental intellectual and moral values falsifies higher education's historical sense of itself. Values, further, can be assessed through critical inquiry. They appropriately can be a direct concern of education in a pluralistic society. When properly understood, the relativity of values presents no barriers to the legitimacy of values education.

Second, values exist as givens at deep and formative levels of personal and social experience. Values exist in, with, and through thinking, doing, and feeling. An education in values offers integrative themes in the critical analysis of human choice and action, and can contribute to the renewal of liberal education and the enhancement of professional education. It provides as well a variety of realistic pedagogical possibilities.

Third, as a unifying aspect of human experience, values provide the possibility of a link between educational form and content, knowledge and conduct, and affect and cognition. A sense of the unity of human consciousness both supports and results from values education.

We have chosen to use the phrase *values education* rather than *moral education* or *ethics,* despite a number of obvious problems. Although the term itself has no clear tradition and invites unwanted comparisons, it accurately reflects our concern with a wide range of human values. While moral education and ethics are mainly concerned with one realm and form of values—moral values, choices, and judgments—as we have seen, there are many other types of values. The broader orientation afforded by values education makes it potentially relevant to virtually every aspect of the academic program. We understand values education to include ethics and moral education. Their role in values education is large because moral values and choices tend to be more central than other values. As we have seen, there is a moral dimension to the rankings that one gives even to personal values, as when one questions the adequacy of one's goals in life. Moreover, political, economic, legal, and social issues typically are not far from the moral sphere, as they often involve questions of justice and human rights. Our choice of terminology will lead, we hope, to greater rather than less clarity, although we are aware that categories of this sort often appear somewhat artificial.

This chapter is intended to provide a general description of the forms of inquiry that are comprised in values education. We do not present a values studies program for any particular topic or field. Rather, we offer theoretical principles—the rationale, the broad aims, and the general methods—through which specific courses and programs could be developed and implemented. We conceive of values education as instruction through a series of interacting and reinforcing forms of inquiry and pedagogy. In practice, they overlap and intertwine, but for the sake of analysis, we can distinguish five pedagogical areas: values analysis, values consciousness, values criticism, values pedagogy, and values development. The first three categories will occupy our attention here, with the final two comprising the subject of the following chapter.

Values Analysis

Values analysis is a form of inquiry by which one seeks to understand the meaning of a human situation through discovering in it the values that orient human choice and decision. The analysis is predicated on the primary assumption that human choice is motivated by an implicit appeal to a set of values—including those that ultimately may prove to be unworthy of being valued because they are false and destructive. Values function as the standards and authorities in the name of which particular goods are known and chosen. As expressions of that which humans love, prize, and cherish, values orient and motivate choice toward satisfaction and fulfillment. An inquiry into values enables one to explore the qualitative dimensions of human experience, to examine a decisive expression of human purposes and goals, of human meaning. Values analysis is an effort to discern what is at stake for human well-being amidst all the richness and complexity of life. To study values is by no means to abandon knowledge and factual analysis, but to illuminate the human purposes and meanings among the facts.

Values analysis is obviously not an esoteric method, to be practiced only by a few initiates. The study of literature, art, history, politics, social relations, philosophy, and religion constantly treat questions of value. Critical inquiry in these fields involves the delineation of values as a way to illuminate an event, a human achievement, an artifact, or a situation. The form and extensiveness of values inquiry in a given critical study depend on whether the researcher's objectives are narrowly disciplinary or broadly humanistic.

In much, though by no means all, of the current practice of many disciplines, even in the humanities, the process of values inquiry has been eroded or excluded. As disciplines have become increasingly quantified and professionalized, their focus has shifted toward a second-order analysis. Each discipline so concentrates on its own special language and literature, its own categories and definitions, and its own methodology, that it easily loses touch with questions of wider human significance. Amitai Etzioni thus describes the decline of humanistic sociology: "undergraduate courses in the methodology of sociology have typically dealt not with the significant issue of how one verifies one's insights into the social world, but with such specialized questions as the relative merits of mailed questionnaires and face-to-face interviews, of quota sampling and statistically random sampling" (1976, p. 32). Robert Gorham Davis offers a similar critique of programs in the humanities, one which emphasizes what the discipline loses as its gaze moves from problems of human life: "If we are serious about fundamental discussions in philosophy, literary criticism, history, and other disciplines, it is because they have bearing, however indirectly, on many aspects of our lives, including the practical. If they do not have such bearing, then these discussions are games, however delightful, and the much-vaunted scholarly rigor is merely a performer's skill, that of a tightropewalker. We watch the performance only if we have a taste for it, as with chess or tennis; if not, we can cheerfully ignore it" (1973, p. 5).

The basic problem that Etzioni and Davis are describing is one that we have met before. For many practitioners of the disciplines, method and perspective have come to define and exhaust the reality of the object under study. If, in other words, a given methodology and its instruments cannot measure a certain phenomenon of human experience, then the practitioner assumes either that the phenomenon does not exist or that it is of no consequence. Such an assumption involves the ironic and radical arbitrariness of presuming that the epistemological needs of a single discipline determine the nature of reality itself. If it cannot be known *this* way, it is not there; or, whatever is there can only be known to the extent that it is pared to fit the instrument at hand. Needless to say, the human consequences—the good and evil—of events often are ignored because they are so difficult to measure and resolve.

Many disciplinary perspectives could be used to exemplify the habits of thought that we are describing here. Behaviorist psychology, especially in the work of B. F. Skinner, provides a militant illustration. The effort to develop a science of behavior involves a "redescription" of the way events are characterized in ordinary language. Many words, behaviorists claim, are pre-scientific and must be translated into scientific terminology. With regard to values, for instance, Skinner asserts that "to make a value judgment by calling something good or bad is to classify it in terms of its reinforcing effects" (1972, p. 99). This redefinition of good and bad results in the following description of values: " 'You should (you ought to) tell the truth' is a value judgment to the extent that it refers to reinforcing contingencies. We might translate it as follows: 'If you are reinforced by the approval of your fellow men, you will be reinforced when you tell the truth.' The value is to be found in the social contingencies maintained for control. It is an ethical or moral judgment in the sense that ethos and mores refer to the customary practices of a group" (1972, p. 107).

That this account be offered as one of many possible descriptions of various aspects of truth telling does not surprise us. In fact, though, Skinner's "translation" is intended as an exhaustive explanation of the human phenomenon of truth telling. For Skinner, the methods and assumptions of behavioral psychology are arbitrarily posited as the only ways *any* question about human experience can be answered. He has taken a methodological scheme and transformed it into a definition of reality.

What, then, are the consequences for education and human affairs if values are ignored or are "translated" into some other kind of reality? Mary Midgely sums up nicely two of the results: "To ignore the multiplicity of [human] wants, and therefore of goods, to talk as though value were a simple one-dimensional quantitative matter, has two bad consequences. First, discussion may become so unreal, so far from any use in understanding our practical problems, that it becomes merely a detached game; we may even pride ourselves on this detachment. Second, we may simply root for our own favored good, our chosen aspect of human life, under the flag of neutral analysis" (1978, p. 191).

A dangerous irony taints those rationalistic and scientific approaches that remove values from the sphere of objectivity and deny their place in education. Such approaches reduce the critical and encompassing choices in a person's or a society's life to so many emotions and impulses. Their proponents tacitly admit that the very decisions on which the quality of human life depends are beyond critical and rational reflection, to be settled by passion or preference, power or persuasion. This admission removes critical intelligence from the inevitable conflict over values and indicates, in effect, that anything goes. But we cannot avoid having to choose among values; choosing is intrinsic to human existence. The result of the approach Midgely decries is that values are chosen inescapably, but often under the guise of neutrality.

Professional education and practice provide parallels with the analytical habits of the disciplines. To study a profession is to learn a certain way of seeing and acting on the world that creates an insular system of hidden, specialized values. There are many contemporary illustrations, but perhaps the most vivid are from the realm of technology. Frequently, technologists unconsciously assume that the needs of a technological system for its own efficiency, growth, and perfection are good for man. Hence the sense of excitement that first greets the fertilization of a human embryo in a test tube, while second thoughts stir doubts and fears. How does one judge whether a process is mere technological wizardry that may lead to inhumane practices or useful for the medical arts of true human healing? We can become so immersed in our professional identities and rituals, in this case the sheer challenge of a medical technique, that we can easily fail to see the hidden and human meaning of our practices.

A clarification and analysis of values can help to provide professionals and laymen with the sensitivity to wider questions of human meaning and obligation that frequently is missing in the disciplines and professions. As an explicit method, values inquiry and analysis can help us explore personal values as well as broader intellectual, esthetic, ethical, social, and political values. In all cases, this analysis compels us to unearth the commitments and claims that stand behind the manifold particulars and possibilities of a given situation. We must study values not as ordinary objects but as patterns of human agency, as the integrative dimensions of human experience in which thought and feeling, purposes and intentions coalesce. One can do this by pressing a characteristic set of questions about any situation: What are the relations between matters of fact and questions of value? What are the patterns and uniformities of choice, and which values give them this particular shape? What priorities do the patterns reveal, and what underlying values and commitments determine the priorities? Which factors are given weight in the situation, and which are excluded? What is or would be sacrificed for the sake of what is assumed to be the greater good? In the name of what authority are choices made and justified? What alternative courses of action are available, and how is the selection made from among them? How are conflicts understood and resolved? What social and intellectual traditions are invoked for support? One is asking, in effect, What is really going on?

Values inquiry is not an isolated technique, cut off from an interest in beliefs, myths, principles, laws, institutions, and factual circumstances. To analyze values is, to be figurative, like finding the center of perspective in a painting toward which all the lines converge, or like locating the focal mass in a gravitational field. The study of values moves beyond itself toward these "lines" and this "field." It might lead us to an extended consideration of the underlying vision of human nature and destiny, or require us to explore the facts more fully. The conclusions that we reach in values analysis require, of course, various types of evidence and warrants, much as in any form of critical inquiry. These conclusions are descriptive statements about what values are present in a situation. They are not specific value judgments that such and such should be done. Values analysis could indeed prepare the way and provide the backing for value judgments, but the latter require a different and distinctive step.

As we have suggested, values analysis is not an esoteric method, but it does require special sensitivities and skills. The aim is not merely to produce a list of basic values like justice, truth, and order, as if somehow these terms themselves possess the magic to reveal the full texture of a situation. Values always exist in relation with other values, both in harmony and conflict. These relations and conflicts must be educed and assessed, and in the process one may discover cross-purposes and contradictions. Then, too, apparent agreement may evolve into conflict, as when the equality of opportunity confronts the equality of result. By searching and pressing for significant and precise distinctions in and among values, we can elicit the tonalities of choice and obligation. We can look, for example, to the work of a thinker like Reinhold Niebuhr, whose political and social writings offer many examples of a searching analysis of values in the context of practical problems. Niebuhr possessed remarkable abilities to describe the intricate dialetical relationships between love and justice, freedom and order, and power and responsibility. The result was not merely a string of bloodless abstractions, but valuable insights into the meaning and possibilities of contemporary history.

The specific possibilities of values analysis in the study of business and corporations is illustrated in these remarks of William C. Frederick: "The study and careful analysis of values will become the centerpiece of all business and society scholarship. Values are what the business and society field is all about. What we witness in confrontations between the corporation and its various social constituencies is a clash of values. Women, blacks and other minorities, youth, the aged, ecologists, consumers, and others are challenging the values that suffuse the corporate enterprise. What is now surely needed—and what we can expect from business and society scholars—is a more carefully and systematically developed understanding of business values and the values of those who maintain that business serves the community less well than it should. How can these competing value systems be compared? How can the apparent inconsistencies be reconciled? What principles can be employed to decide between clashing values? What social mechanisms of compromise, accommodation, and resolution can be brought into play?" (1977, pp. 16–17).

These comments exemplify how values analysis can provide a superb interdisciplinary theme for liberal and professional education. Each of the disciplines in the social sciences and the humanities is concerned with values in one way or another, and can shed a different light on the topic. The study of values can provide a meeting place for various fields where theoretical issues and the pressing problems of real life are studied together. As Frederick states, "We need a breakthrough that will enable us to see that values belong to all, that they arise out of human [and] cultural experience, and that understanding them is everyone's business and not to be restricted to experts, philosophers, or professional moralizers. Values—and value inquiry—belong in the public domain" (1977, p. 17).

We have stressed that in itself values analysis is a descriptive intellectual method. It corrects a narrowness in contemporary thinking by focusing on the question of worth, but in itself it does not try to prescribe specific choices. It foreshadows the capability of values education to affect conduct, although it does not itself aim directly at altering behavior. One can expect that a responsible person will be significantly influenced by the disclosure of values that have been previously hidden, and by the discovery of contradictions in both personal and social values. To reveal values is to unveil claims and obligations. For persons of goodwill, the discovery of relevant values sets the stage for acting on them.

Values Consciousness

Values analysis leads to another moment in values education —values consciousness. In one sense, of course, any analysis of values results in one's awareness of them. But a particular type of consciousness, one that can be vivid and affecting, is exemplified in one's awareness of one's own values and of those of the institutions in whose life one shares. Awareness, in this sense, is no passive mental register. It is consciousness as self-consciousness, mediated through an active "making present" of the values that shape one's own decisions and behavior. Nor is the potency of the awareness of values limited to direct personal experience. Through the powers of imagination, the foreign, the distant, and the absent can be brought near. By focusing on values, our imagination and sensitivity can re-create the struggles, intensities, and passions that surround choices as they are made and lives as they are lived.

Values consciousness makes it possible for us to recapture some of the sense of importance and drama with which people feel, think, choose, and act. Our awareness of values gives us a way not only to know, but to experience, the meaning of our humanity.

The potential power of values consciousness, especially as self-consciousness, requires little proof in the contemporary world. We see on all sides social and cultural revolutions based on changes in a people's consciousness. These include violent political transformations as well as the deeply reverberating social changes impelled by the movements for racial and sexual equality. In the words of Paulo Freire, "A deepened consciousness of their situation leads men to apprehend that situation as an historical reality susceptible of transformation" (1970, p. 73).

These dramatic changes illustrate the underlying dynamic of the personal awareness of values. As the self discovers its own values, it truly finds itself. One discovers one's human identity, where one stands, what one counts for, and what counts for one. Through values awareness, one poses basic questions about one's purposes and loyalties, one's sources of worth and self-respect. The experience can be painful, leading to anger and rebellion, for the self may find that its own deepest needs for self-esteem and self-expression have been slighted or denied. Strong feelings—fears and hopes, loves and hates, joys and sorrows—are not denied or repressed in values consciousness, but are respected as indices of human meaning. They are interpreted and made intelligible by the presence of values. In more quiescent and prosaic contexts, too, values consciousness works in a similar way, disclosing to the participants in a decision or a conflict the human meaning of the situation.

Our era often suffers from glaring failures in moral consciousness and imagination, from the loss of the power to bring to full personal presence the human meaning of our actions. If, for instance, the various Watergate memoirs share a common thread, it is that of Nixon's men tangling themselves in hopeless compromises with simple truth and honesty, unconscious of the tribal morality that they had adopted. Hannah Arendt's memorable phrase "the banality of evil" suggests that powerful systems, technologies, and bureaucracies develop routines that have a morally blind life of their own. The individual's conscience may become trapped by parochial boundaries or caught up in business as usual, the result of which is a deadening of the personal experience of human good and evil.

The need and the opportunity for education to contribute to values awareness are real, but the challenge is equally great. On the one hand, values education must confront the prevailing model of knowledge as objective, impersonal, instrumental, specialized, reductionistic, atomistic, and amoral (Harrison, 1978). A concern for empathy, sensitivity, vision, caring, and personal presence find little place within conventional educational wisdom. On the other hand, values education must cope with the persistent human tendencies simply to forget or to deny the full context of choice in order to concentrate on the immediacies of life. Hidden enabling structures like values fall outside the conscious pragmatic focus of life. They are so much and deeply with us, that special steps are necessary to unearth them. Jacob Neusner describes the pragmatism and emotional numbness of contemporary students: "What strikes me about our students, when we first meet them, is how limited is their range of emotions, their expectations of themselves. Having endured and survived the terrible trial of adolescence, they huddle together, bound within in their own flat and narrow circle of permissible aspirations of career, not character. It is as if surviving is all that can be asked of humanity. Striking out on one's own is dangerous and demands courage. Imagination is for fools. Anguish, failure, self-doubt are to be dulled. Tears and laughter are permitted only in careful measure about some few things" (1979, p. 40).

When pursued in the context of these issues, values consciousness offers the promise of linking vigorous knowledge with the depths of human feeling. It presents itself again as an integrative enterprise. A consciousness of values often depends essentially on the ability to empathize with another's dilemma, to enter that person's life. The presence of values may be brought to awareness precisely through sharing another's feelings of joy and fulfillment or of sorrow and suffering. The full understanding of an august value like justice finally depends upon a *sense* of justice; it requires a sensitive emotional compass. For example, decision making in medical ethics about questions of life and death must be more than an intellectual calculus. Such deliberations require of us the ability to portray to ourselves and others the emotional meaning of a decision—its effects on the real lives of real people who have financial burdens, job responsibilities, and family ties.

As feelings reveal the color and temper of the values that are present, they can be faithful guides to the meaning that an experience has for those who live through it. Neusner compares meaning derived from emotion and that from intellect in this way: "in the enhancement of our capacities to imagine, to transcend ourselves and enter into the being of others, I think the beginning lies in the imagination of potentialities of emotion and sentiment. For not all will ever see or hear or think about thought, but everyone has sentiment and heart. All bury and are buried, love and are loved. None ever passed through life without that: the experience of life and death" (1979, p. 40).

But, we know too that feelings can overwhelm a situation, can reject all bounds, can feed on themselves, and provide no sure ground for choice and action. At this point, values awareness offers normative limits by circumscribing the significance of emotion to its revelation of the human good. It is precisely the capacity of emotions to disclose the human good or evil of a decision that gives feeling and its expressions the authority that they can possess. Feelings that do not disclose values sink toward insignificance or unintelligibility, at least in terms of choice and action. They become, then, primarily a matter of psychological interest.

How one goes about fostering values consciousness through education is, of course, no simple matter. As we shall note later, certain subjects and themes are especially effective. In virtually any field, though, an awareness of values can be heightened by pressing the inquiry in characteristic ways. One must look below the surface of events and question the patterns of ordinary analysis. David Bohm stresses the importance of insight, which he defines as "an *act,* permeated by intense passion, that makes possible great clarity in the sense that it perceives and dissolves subtle but strong emotional, social, linguistic, and intellectual pressures tending to hold the mind in rigid grooves and fixed compartments, in which fundamental challenges are avoided" (1979, p. 409).

The metaphors of sight and vision introduced by Bohm reveal several aspects of values analysis and consciousness. The plane of values is not reached by adding new facts to existing information, but by seeing what is there in new ways. As in vision, a different pattern suddenly can emerge from the familiar. We become aware of the situation, or see it, in a different light. Suddenly we understand the passion and intensity, the striving and sacrifice that had appeared as so many odd facts. When values consciousness becomes self-conscious, one grasps oneself as a person, and as a certain kind of person, as an agent engaged in responsible relations with other persons in a context of choice and values. At whatever level of thought or action one's new vision penetrates, it finds already present one's given pattern of values: the loyalties and loves, dreams and aspirations, demands and obligations that define one's unique and personal presence in the world. These are the commitments and goals that each person relies upon, sometimes desperately and usually anxiously, for his or her own sense of adequacy and purpose. Intensity, care, and drama surround these self-investing choices: the intensity of being who one is, the care that accompanies the hidden pull of integrity, and the drama that surrounds the possibility of losing or gaining one's self. To envision and to reveal values at this level involve a strong and stirring experience of self. Who, then, am I to be and to act in these ways? This question hovers over the process of awareness and explains the unconditional seriousness with which the answers often come.

In metaphoric language, the inability to see one's values is a form of blindness. In one sense, this blindness is understandable since one's values are so intimate that one can easily overlook them. They so define the nature of personal intention and agency that they may disappear behind everyday choices and tasks. Roger Mehl uses the metaphor of the loss of the sight in this way: "The disappearance of values from the field of our vision is tied to an error of perspective: to the extent that we plane off the surface of the world, to the extent that our attention to the nuances of colors, to the intensities of lights, weakens, our perception of values weakens" (1957, p. 44, my translation).

The metaphor of sight captures several, but not all, aspects of values consciousness. We need to learn not only to see values, but to articulate what they mean for us. This articulation is a skill that can be taught and learned, as Herbert Fingarette argues: "To become explicitly conscious of something is to be exercising a certain skill. Skills, of course, are learned but need not be routinized. We are born with certain general capacities which we shape, by learning, into specific skills, some of them being quite sensitive and artful. The specific skill I particularly have in mind as a model for becoming explicitly conscious of something is the skill of saying what we are doing or experiencing. I propose, then, that we do not characterize consciousness as a kind of mental mirror, but as the exercise of the (learned) skill of 'spelling out' some feature of the world we are engaged in" (1969, pp. 38–39).

An awareness of values, like other forms of self-awareness, can be learned through a process of comparison and contrast. One's discovery of self is often initiated by the discovery of the other. An individual's identity takes form only once he defines himself as separate from his parents. We become aware of the specific qualities that our way of life possesses when we contrast it with others. Perhaps one of the clearest methods for pursuing values awareness in this vein is the process of challenge and response. When students are asked to state what they believe and why, when they are asked to indicate where they stand, when pressed to defend a position, their consciousness of values is heightened. As Kohlberg's and others' work suggests, tolerant and supportive "disequilibrium" can markedly enhance a person's moral self-awareness.

This approach holds that values consciousness occurs when education is made personal, when education is addressed to the structures of personal experience—to the person as a subject. This does not mean that the student's or the instructor's biography is made central, or that education becomes anecdotal. Rather, the instructor directly asks students to become conscious of the sources of their own agonies and satisfactions, and what these represent in the wider world. What is so important to you that it could never be sacrificed for another end? Anything? What seems to count more as you review events and study policies, order or freedom? What cast of mind do you bring to the resolution of social problems—a problem-solving and pragmatic spirit or an ideological and systematic one? This form of personal inquiry is not limited to the individual's own immediate values. So, for example, it is useful to have students imagine what it would be like to experience a certain moral dilemma; to imagine the emotions of the participants and the full range of consequences of the decision; or, to develop in detail the world view of a culture different from their own. The effort to put oneself in another's skin, to assume another point of view, to enter imaginatively another time or world all foster the emergence of values consciousness. The method of using personal queries and responses to promote knowledge was sanctioned by Socrates; values education adapts this inexhaustible technique to focus even more sharply than he did on values as qualifications of the self. Values awareness embraces the classical belief that self-knowledge is the beginning of wisdom.

Before concluding our discussion of values consciousness, we should explore the capacity of values education to influence conduct. We have examined this relationship between education and conduct in our review of other approaches. At this juncture we cannot consider all facets of this important question; we reserve a comprehensive discussion of the changes in students' values effected by values education for later. Here, our goal is to explore some aspects of the relationship between one's awareness of the values one already holds and action. More importantly, we examine closely some assumptions about the way values exist that are implicit in our interpretation of values.

As we have seen, values exist as demands—through establishing an aura of requiredness in the choice among alternatives, by providing an immanent standard of reference and judgment for human self-enactment. Correspondingly, values function as goals, guiding the self and institutions toward what is desired or cherished: In both ways, as demands and as goals, values are necessarily and integrally tied to choice and action, and to the self's constant process of self-appraisal. One does not fully hold a value, then, unless one's action (in the broad sense of the term) is affected by it, and no meaningful action is taken except in the name of some value (or disvalue). Of particular significance here is the way in which knowledge, beliefs, and attitudes—in contrast to values—can easily be suspended, rationalized, or contradicted in action and ignored in self-evaluation. For instance, knowing an ethical princi-ple, acknowledging it as true, does not in itself mean that one will act on it. In most models that seek to explain human action, both those proposed by social scientists and philosophers, there is no logical contradiction in thinking in one way but acting in another. In fact, many contemporary behavioral scientists posit this split as a premise and offer elaborate explanations of why and how it occurs.

With values, however, the case is different. Values constitute part of the self's identity as a human being—not merely as a psychological, or sociological, or political, or even philosophical being. One's values determine the way one puts one's life together; they regulate one's choices and actions, and they are the standards against which one measures one's actions. As the self's standards, they are tied to the forms of self-relatedness and self-consciousness that existence as a self entails. A primordial link exists, then, between one's values and one's critical self-appraisal and self-judgment, between values and conscience. Conscience measures, evaluates, and judges in terms of standards supplied by values; self-questioning and self-rejection ensue if its norms have been violated. The connection between the self and values, which pro-vides values with their base in reality, is transacted and enforced by conscience, that is, by the self in its constitutive role as self-critic. One's intended and chosen values can, of course, be overpowered or altered, but conscience negotiates the process of change and may demand a strenuous justification. Failing to be satisfied, con-science has sanctions, chiefly self-rejection, which may, depending on the person and the culture, be tied to a vast array of self-punishing emotions.

The intensity that we discovered to arise from values consciousness is further explained by this fundamental connection between values and conscience. Unlike knowledge, at least as un-derstood in most perspectives, action is integral to values. One does not hold a value except as one acts on it. Further, values are en-forced by conscience. The self evaluates itself in terms of its faith-fulness to values as its own standards of being and choosing. A clear consciousness of values is, then, a further spur to action. One's commitment to a general path of action appears sharper and more focused, and one discovers new implications and new responsibilities. To be made alive to one's values is to receive a mandate and a call to new possibilities of action. Both in holding values, and in becoming more deeply conscious of them, we close one form of the gap between knowing and doing.

By way of conclusion and transition, it is important that we comment further on the theme of conscience. It might seem foolhardy to propose for it this sort of a central interpretive and educational role. The term has lost much of its meaning in the contemporary world, and often what it retains is trivial and negative. In this context, however, conscience is not some internal nay-sayer or guilt-ridden part of the self. It is one form of self-consciousness, the self in its capacity for critical self-assessment, both in self-affirmation and self-rejection. Conscience is simply one form of consciousness, a relationship made explicit in French, in which the same word is used to refer to both. The intricate psychological dimensions of conscience as internalized approvals and disapprovals of parents and society, and as feelings of guilt and remorse, do not exhaust the human and ethical reality of conscience as critical self-awareness. The force and reality of conscience continue to appear as a structure of consciousness, regardless of the various guilt feelings and self-punishing acts that may be involved. These feelings and internalized approvals and disapprovals of significant others embody and mediate values as the norms of conscience. To discover the values that serve as the criteria for self-assessment, that motivate feelings of guilt or affirmation, is an essential step in values consciousness.

In discussing conscience, we are focusing on the moral dimension of self-evaluation, but this does not require us to turn away from the full range of values. Conscience, as a potent form of self-relationship, serves well to illustrate many aspects of all critical self-consciousness as transacted through values. Further, the forms of self-criticism encompassed by conscience are extremely broad. We meet again the fact that moral experience includes not only the content of explicitly moral issues, but the form of many matters that in themselves are morally neutral. The construction of nuclear power plants, for example, poses technological and economic questions but, particularly after the Three Mile Island accident, most of the discussions about them include value questions that have a strong moral component. Whenever an essential aspect of human possibility as such is at stake, self-evaluation assumes the characteristic forms of self-rejection or self-affirmation that we associate with conscience.

Values Criticism

Both values analysis and values consciousness are descriptive procedures. Through values analysis, we study the values inherent in a situation but do not choose among them. Values consciousness leads us to an awareness of values, whatever they may be. These descriptive procedures provide evidence of another dimension in the total process of values education. Once we have analyzed and clarified the values in a given situation, we often discover conflicts and even contradictions within the same personal or social system. As we become aware of our values, we often make or wish to make significant changes in them. Rather than leaving these contradictions unchallenged and changes unexplained, we need to consider the place of values criticism as a dimension of values education.

The purposes and methods of values criticism are summarized briefly here to provide the agenda for the discussion that follows. Values criticism is a process of inquiry that poses normative questions about the choice and implementation of values, while not itself prescribing specific answers. The questions are normative because they arise from general criteria that are tacitly present in valuing as a form of human consciousness. Values criticism elicits, structures, and applies objective questions that have normative force in the critique of human values. As such, it is a subject appropriate to the mission and responsibilities of the university. Through the force and relevance of this critical process, values criticism addresses and stimulates change in the given content of the students' values. The ultimate pedagogical aim of values criticism is to develop in students an internalized capacity for the constructive self-criticism of values, that is, to educate conscience. It is able, thereby, to link knowledge and action.

The fact that there are general criteria with which to assess values—standards for our standards—is what empowers values criticism as an educational method. How can these general and tacit criteria be found, and what are they?

The first step in locating them is to consider what primary conditions have to pertain for values to exist. Of course, there must be some center, some point of reference or being, for whom the values have worth, whose welfare is enhanced by means of them. We have referred variously to this center as the human person or, more specifically, to values as standards of human agency. Although one could select another starting point, we believe that from this one we attain a suggestive and illuminating perspective from which to assess our experience of values. We can next ask which fundamental features of the self, as an agent, serve as the prerequisites or conditions of possibility for the existence of values. In other words, from observing the way that values actually do exist and function—given their indubitable and necessary presence in establishing a meaningful world—we can infer certain things that the self must *be, do,* and *have.* By examining people's submission to the authority of values, we can extrapolate several characteristics that humans possess. We see at least three conditions as necessary dimensions of human consciousness for valuing to occur as it in fact does: freedom, responsibility, and respect. These characteristics refer to fundamental traits of persons, not simply to their specific acts.

First, human consciousness possesses freedom to act, freedom as agency. The freedom in question is not simply freedom from casual control or coercion, as in most debates over freedom of the will, but is the fundamental capacity for human initiative and self-determination. This freedom constitutes the human power to change or master a situation, to overcome limits through truth and knowledge, action and creativity, and to relate and be present to another person. Values are precisely the standards of and for this freedom, giving shape and order to human choice. Without human choice, without the capacity for self-determination, valuing would not be possible. Freedom is an immanent condition of valuing.

Second, responsibility is the pattern of human agency. This responsibility is not a casual notion that refers simply to a person's having to answer for his actions, but is a global image of human agency. H. Richard Niebuhr offers this definition: "The idea or pattern of responsibility . . . may summarily be defined as the idea of an agent's action as response to an action upon him in accordance with his expectation of response to his response; and all of this in a continuing community of agents" (1963, p. 65). Without responsibility as a condition, values would not have the characteristic continuities and patterns that they do. If values were only fragmentary, momentary, and discontinuous, they could not link human possibility with the continuities of the world, nor be the values of the same self.

Third, respect is the content of human agency. People's values are founded on respect, basic acceptance, and affirmation both of self and others. Since all values seek to realize and advance the good of the self, they obviously are posited on a basic self-affirmation or self-respect. Respect for the other is simultaneously given, too, since self-affirmation entails affirmation by others. The two forms of respect are constituitively reciprocal.

Having defined these qualities of the agent, we now can elicit the tacit criteria of valuing. At this point, we ask what values have to be, what conditions of possibility they are required to satisfy, what criteria they must meet, in order to be the values of human agency as responsibility, freedom, and respect. This dialectical or circular method is warranted since we start with values as givens, as necessary forms of human presence in the world, and not simply as possibilities of thought. The criteria of valuing, these standards of our standards, emerge through the continuing interaction of human agents, one with another, with general forms of logical reasoning, and with the world at large. We know that values provide the general conditions for the self's action in the world. The present task is to break the experience of valuing into smaller domains of meaning and obligation.

The criteria of valuing are tacit in the sense that they are given implicitly in ordinary experience, and they are reflected in ordinary language. We will elicit them here in an informal way, although it would be possible to develop them in a propositional framework. Although elements of a philosophical theory will be used, the development of an exhaustive philosophical argument is not our present goal. Our aim is twofold: to illustrate how values criticism has a basic connection with ordinary experience and to show how the criteria of valuing are objective and necessary, if tacit, dimensions of that same experience. We will fulfill our goals by examining many commonplace expressions, judgments, questions, and experiences. Ordinary experience and language, and the assumptions that stand behind them reveal the presence of the criteria. Using these criteria, values education can then work with and through various academic disciplines and formally extract, articulate, systematize, and apply the tests and questions that reality itself already harbors. Our analysis yields eight criteria of values, which we now define.

Consistency: We can and do ask constantly, and often pointedly, whether a person's beliefs are consistent with his or her actions, whether actions at one time are consistent with those at another, and whether two values in the same system are consistent. When an individual discovers genuine contradictions in and among his values, as in and among propositions, such dissonance motivates a change in values to eliminate the incongruity (see Rokeach, 1973). Consistency has another form as well—in its more abstract role as the principle of generalizability. What if everyone did that? is a commonplace question that reveals the presence of the test of practical consistency in everyday life. As we have seen, its systematic use in ethics is well-established.

Reciprocity: Reciprocity is a form of consistency, as illustrated in the common refrain, How would you like it if I treated you like that? Valuing carries within itself both the rational test of consistency and the prerequisite of respect for self and others. These are merged in the test of reciprocity, which has its classical expression in the Golden Rule.

Coherence: Values, both personal and cultural ones, form coherent systems or constellations. We can and do ask in a variety of contexts "what sense things make" through and in the relations among values. Coherence describes the integration of values into a system or code. What justifies the value rankings that we adopt in our lives, our passion for certain values over others? Is there proportionality or fanaticism, orderliness or randomness, justification or arbitrariness? We constantly reason about values in terms of tacit appeals to points of reference like these. Not every pattern of choice among values fits intelligibly together, and those that do not may fail to meet the test of coherence.

Comprehensiveness: Comprehensiveness is a test that challenges the meaning of a self-contained value system by asking it to encounter a wider circle of reality. Through experience, we find that our way of life needlessly cuts us off from other groups and is not broad enough to give meaning to other people's histories. As our relationships broaden from family to neighborhood, from neighborhood to larger geographical and cultural areas, we often discover the narrowness and restrictiveness of our values. Internal coherence and consistency can be established around small social units like the family or the neighborhood.

Adequacy: A presupposition of our valuing is the achievement of human meaning, the solving of problems, and the overcoming of obstacles. We therefore never cease to ask of a given effort, Does it work? Does the idea fit, is the problem solved, are people truly understanding one another? Have the actual needs of human beings been addressed effectively? To be adequate, values must reflect the presupposition of all valuing—the basic respect of self and others. Our ordinary language is filled with the convincing indicators of inadequacy—destructiveness, suffering, error, isolation, failure, and defeat. Having demonstrated these results, any argument is won.

Duration: Values that are adequate and comprehensive with respect to time meet the criterion of duration. Time is a fundamental dimension of human experience that shapes, challenges, and tests our choices in countless ways. It shows up in the most ordinary exchanges, "that just won't last," and provides as well a way to measure the significance of exalted works of human creativity. Literature, folklore, and religion warn and advise in a thousand simple and profound ways to meet well the test of time. Transience is a deadly foe. Is the prize worth the effort? Will the victory last or is it fleeting? In this criterion, and in those related to it, we see clearly the presence of human agency as responsibility.

Authenticity: A condition of valuing is self-determination, requiring that my values be *my* values. Trying to hold values simply through conformity to the standards of others is inauthentic and ultimately impossible. Is that what *you* really believe? is an unsettling and telling question, especially for those unsure of their own value commitments, and hence of themselves.

Openness. Many of the foregoing criteria depend procedurally on the test of openness, the willingness to at least listen to the other side, to evaluate another viewpoint. One's values do not fulfill the condition of responsibility as a pattern of human agency if one's process of valuing is closed and rigid. The ability to respond to change, to entertain alternative points of view, and to cope with new circumstances are tests to which we subject our values.

The type of critical inquiry that is illustrated here points to the numerous possibilities for a fully developed method of values criticism within higher education. From these points of departure, a class could move toward a more structured and systematic critique of values in a variety of curricular areas. The actual form of the inquiry—the specific questions that are posed—depends on whether the analysis and criticism of values is directed toward the cultural ethos, public policy, social and historical issues, the nature of the good life, legal issues, professional responsibility, ethical dilemmas, and so forth. Each field, from art history to economics, will have characteristic ways of adapting and relating values inquiry to its own methods, literature, and subject matter. The testing of values will bear a threefold imprint: that of the academic field, the topic at hand, and the criteria of valuing. It will occur at a variety of levels of generality, depending again on the material that is being studied. Values criticism reorients and extends critical inquiry in the disciplines. When values criticism is directed toward a specific choice between competing actions, as in applied ethics, it embraces a determination of factual conditions and a consideration of relevant principles and rules of conduct. In many cases, inconsistency, incoherence, inadequacy, disrespect, and so forth can be determined only by specific arguments and judgments. Ethical argumentation is one of the prominent forms of values criticism, addressed to particular principles, cases, and decisions. As we have emphasized before, values always are linked to accompanying forms of human consciousness including, of course, specific ethical judgments. As part of values criticism, however, ethical principles and rules would reflect clearly their origin in underlying human values as forms of moral experience.

As an objective method, values criticism is fully consistent with the role of colleges and universities in a pluralistic society. It is able to deal with significant human concerns in a way that avoids indoctrination and partisanship, moralism and special pleading. It uses a rigorous methodology that is generally applicable, but does not prescribe the specific content of an individual's or a group's value system. The possibility of indoctrination is remote since values criticism helps students develop precisely those skills necessary to resist indoctrination; it teaches students to interrogate every claimant to truth or authority. Values criticism promotes skills for choice and freedom.

Values criticism, unlike some of the approaches we earlier investigated, is not empty or relativistic. Its principal achievement would be for students to internalize, to make permanently part of themselves, basic forms of critical self-assessment and social appraisal. The critique of values provides one's individual and social conscience with an objective set of reference points to test any value or set of values. It seeks to make conscious, articulate, and potent the hidden tests that experience itself provides for any value. Its questions are telling and effective because they create an encounter between conscience and the objective norms of human agency.

Values criticism can be seen as paralleling, and even extending, the goals which many would claim are central in all academic training. Higher learning typically prizes its capacity to develop students' powers and habits of critical intelligence. We strive to teach students how to think, not what to think. In similar ways, colleges and universities can foster students' ability to value carefully and critically, leaving to the individuals the final responsibility for what they will value.

Values criticism is a process that can affect the content of one's values. Conscience no doubt hears first the voices of its immediate social and psychological context, but it recognizes other calls as well. How else can we explain the significant changes that occur through heightened awareness of values, or the way persons frequently transcend and reject the norms of their immediate group, or the doubt and hesitancy that surround most decisions? Conscience not only judges—it also questions, searches, and evaluates. Conscience not only applies existing standards, it submits, or can submit, those standards to a critical test. The stability that it provides is not insulated against change. Conscience, after all, is a form of consciousness, with attendant broad powers of apprehension, knowledge, and criticism. Its inevitable immediacies are simultaneously immersed in a wider quest for meaning, integrity, vindication, and worth. Conscience is coextensive with the self's agency as responsibility, freedom, and respect and with its total experience of meaning and purpose. Values criticism can help us explore the dynamics of this process, holding forth to the self that is, the self that might be. Conscience can be liberated, in a precise sense of the term, through education. Its petty tyrannies can be summoned to trial by the insistent demands of human freedom, its acts of self-punishment must come before the supreme court of human self-respect, and its narrow loyalties are judged by the laws of the universal commonwealth of human responsibility. The critical issue regarding conscience is how local or universal is the tribunal in which it takes its stand. This context determines the questions that the self asks of itself.

We have described values criticism as predicated on the broadest characteristics of human agency in order to clarify its general features and minimal possibilities. There are, of course, a number of determinative and more specific value systems within which we all live. Two of fundamental importance to the university are the constellation of democratic values and the enabling intellectual and moral values of the academic community itself. Each of these broad regions offers opportunities for values education and formation that avoid indoctrination and moralistic prescription. Democratic and academic values are articulations of human agency and do not violate its conditions, so the general criteria and critical apparatus remain relevant. If one adds to the general criteria specific criteria relevant to the particular value system, the process of values assessment suggested here can be applied to intellectual or democratic codes of values. We shall explore later how colleges and universities can discharge the responsibilities that they have in these and other spheres.

At this point it has become clear that an approach to values education as analysis, consciousness, and criticism provides a legitimate basis for affirming or for seeking changes in values. Change could come in many forms: in the replacement of one value with another, through new ways of implementing the same value, by raising or lowering the importance of a value in relation to others.

In whatever form, the changes would arise from the challenges that a person experiences when he analyzes and attains a critical awareness of his values. As one reveals the contradictions, incoherence, narrowness, inauthenticity, rigidity, inadequacy, or destructiveness of one's values (or disvalues), one's conscience compels one to move in new directions. Conscience is able to provide what the mind alone lacks, the capacity to disturb, convict, and enforce. Conscience is the self's severe yet benign power to affirm or to reject itself. Values education thus can provide the basis for changes in values, which then motivate changes in behavior.

-»»-»»-»» *Five* «-««-««

Curriculum and
Campus Strategies

-»»-»»-»»-»»-»» -»»«-««-««-««-««-««-««-««

Taken together, values analysis, consciousness, and criticism define a broad method of inquiry and assessment. The integration of values education into the college curriculum would require significant, but not radical, changes in current forms of teaching and learning within higher education. Many college teachers have for years used methods and achieved results broadly parallel to those we have discussed. Whenever students are deeply engaged with important ideas and values, their education leaves an enduring influence on their lives. Further, instructors of many existing courses in liberal and professional education could easily focus more sharply on questions of broad human significance, thereby significantly enhancing values education. In many ways, our analysis is as much a statement of what sometimes happens in education as it is a proposal for what should happen. Nevertheless, educators need to make a systematic and conscious commitment to fostering values through appropriate and imaginative forms of pedagogy. Among other things, it is important to seek to end the divorce between educational form and content, between the techniques and the subject matter of values education. In this chapter, we discuss how values education can grant equal and simultaneous attention to both the content and form of the curriculum.

Values Pedagogy

Our discussion of values analysis, consciousness, and criticism, and our earlier review of the various proposals for moral education and the teaching of values and ethics, have revealed important strategies and subjects for values education. Our aim now is to enter the realm of practice and to apply some of the methods that we have presented. At the outset, it is clear that values analysis, consciousness, and criticism cannot be a passive affair based solely on the transmission of information. As basic conditions, values pedagogy requires that students:

- Be active in developing and defending their own positions
- Be challenged to probe deeply the justifications for human choices, especially their own
- Confront standards and points of view that counter their personal perspectives
- Be encouraged and enabled to assume the role of someone with a contrasting point of view
- Wrestle with problems that have no simple solutions

The content of values education is not defined by a specific subject matter, although certain topics and approaches are especially appropriate. Students should study fields and topics that lead them to consider the tone, texture, and motivation of human action and experience; choices that have significant consequences for the quality of human life; competing points of view that represent plausible alternatives. Such discussions should include both practical and theoretical issues and arguments. An ample literature should be available with a sufficient basis in fact, theory, and criticism.

Taking these guidelines as a starting-point, we can sketch several broad curricular possibilities for the study of values.

Social Choices and Cultural Issues. The future of society, critical social choices, and the quality of life are general themes that encompass a variety of conflicts and issues. Courses that treat social problems could be taught by a team of scholars from different backgrounds to engage the issues that no one field can grasp fully. Students would evaluate the competing alternative solutions by revealing the values they represent. Dozens of possibilities for topical study, often using case histories, arise in history, public policy, law, international relations, science and technology, environmental protection, human rights, economics, and so forth. The courses would not merely provide a running commentary on public events, but would require students to analyze and evaluate the underlying values and dilemmas in social and cultural choice. This focus on values provides an organizing theme that would give interdisciplinary work the clear focus it so often lacks.

Consider, as one example, a course or a section of a course on constitutional law and the issue of race. The case materials could include landmark decisions like *Plessy* v. *Ferguson, Brown* v. *the Topeka Board of Education,* and *Bakke* v. *the Board of Regents of the University of California.* These decisions involve far more than just technical explications of law. They propose basic interpretations of democracy and of human morality and existence. The issues and the decisions could be probed effectively through the methods of values education. That different values often underlie legal and moral reflection might indeed be one of the major conclusions of such an inquiry. As a topic in values studies, the cases illustrate the heart of the meaning of democratic values like equality, freedom, and justice. Students could pursue questions regarding the relation between race and human identity, between social conditions and human dignity, in relevant psychological, political, sociological, and philosophical literature. They could explore difficult value conflicts such as those between equality of opportunity and equality of result in changing historical contexts, from "separate but equal" to affirmative action. In response to their positions on the cases, students could investigate their own values for consistency, coherence, adequacy, reciprocity, openness, and authenticity. What situations issue from considering race a defining human characteristic? Can racism be justified through a coherent and consistent intellectual position? What could happen if everyone's legal rights were a function of race? Does an individual have a personal right to be racist? Values education allows a disciplined form of inquiry on an important subject to be integrated with an affecting experience of self-evaluation.

This one illustration reveals, too, the way that the study of values in a specific case leads of its own weight to wider questions that cut across and pull together the various disciplines. To study the issue of racial discrimination is also to explore the meaning of human dignity, which in turn leads to fundamental questions about the nature of human experience. This same natural movement of thought from the particular to the general can be traced in countless other value-laden issues. By following this movement, we can organize our curriculums along the principles of the core concepts and values of human experience, a pattern that provides continuity and coherence in an otherwise fragmented course of study.

Normative and Professional Ethics. The recent emphases in ethics on substantive issues in social policy and on professional and applied ethics, provide ample and obvious possibilities for values education. Ethical argumentation and analysis of actual decisions and cases provide one model for discourse in values analysis and criticism. Courses in values education can include the study of contemporary ethicists' work on the determination of right conduct and questions of social and professional responsibility. Our earlier study of trends in the teaching of ethics provides a number of illustrations of the types of value questions and issues that are raised in courses in applied and professional ethics.

The Good Life. If applied ethics typically deals with issues of specific obligation, "the good life" suggests a concern for questions of aspiration and virtue. What kind of life do I choose to lead? What will be my values and priorities as a person? Contemporary philosophy has almost totally abandoned an interest in this area, although it can be of critical importance at various turning points in an individual's life. Students can effectively explore questions of virtue and life-style by analyzing literary, dramatic, religious, and philosophic works and applying the techniques of values criticism.

A course in which, for example, students read philosophical, religious, and literary texts would stimulate them to consider different versions of the good life. They could explore the value of integrity by studying Plato's account of Socrates' death in the *Crito* alongside Bolt's moving play about Thomas More, *A Man for All Seasons.* Aristotle's arguments in the *Ethics* for happiness as the practice of contemplative reason, or Plato's in the *Republic,* could be contrasted with Skinner's version of behavioral happiness in *Walden Two.* Arthur Miller's portrait of Willie Loman's desperate pursuit of success in the *Death of a Salesman* could be read accompanied by Maslow's notions of a hierarchy of personal values. The images of power and authority found in George McGregor Burns' *Leadership* could be compared with those in dramatic and literary works like *Hamlet, The Emperor Jones,* or *Moby Dick.* Endless possibilities exist for using the methods of critical values inquiry to test the models offered in the readings as well as the students' own emerging philosophies of life. Do they meet the criticisms and challenges to which they are subject? Will the satisfactions that a model promises endure? Does the proposed way of life create harmony or friction with other people? Do the benefits accrue to the individual alone or does a wider community share in them? Such inquiry structures a pattern of reflection about an intrinsically important subject matter and compels students to address directly crucial choices in their lives and those of others.

Comparative Cultural Studies. The nearly exclusive emphasis on Western culture in undergraduate education continues, even after many efforts to change it. Cross-cultural studies would both correct this narrowness and contribute to students' education in values. Comparative studies of other cultures—their law, ethics, social policies and relations, and religion—enable students to better understand the contours of their own culture. There is perhaps no better way to grasp the full implications of one's values than by coming to understand other ways of life. Courses in anthropology and other social sciences offer students some glimpses of other cultures, but these courses usually do not emphasize values consciousness and criticism.

The relationship between technology and changes in values is an especially fruitful theme for cross-cultural study and comparison. Nations in many parts of the world are trying to pursue a program of technological modernization while protecting their traditional cultural and religious values. The resulting tension and turmoil can often be explained by analyzing the clash of technological and traditional values. Values analysis, consciousness, and criticism enable students to perceive the dynamics of this conflict and to anticipate the problems that result during a period of rapid change.

The Moral Imagination. Values consciousness has a superb ally in the arts. They appeal to our imagination, to our power to make present what is absent, to experience the meaning and weigh the consequences of human action. Without imagination and empathy, human choice can go badly awry—even when one has clarified the theoretical issues. Music, literature, film, drama, and the visual arts offer us countless possibilities to foster our values consciousness and to sharpen our moral imagination.

Beyond contributing to the development of the imagination—a power essential in moral life and judgment—artistic works are able to disclose the meaning of a human situation with all the texture that it has for those who experience it. The arts powerfully reveal the human stakes of value choices. We do not mean to suggest that art offers specific moral lessons or gives tidy exhortations. Rather, that in creating their art, artists must grapple seriously in their own way with issues of consequence in human experience. Courses in values education can and should look to the arts as an important resource.

Experiential Learning and Career Preparation. The present effort to increase the students' opportunities for practical experience, often including preprofessional internships, is another occasion for values education. These provide the opportunity for students to test their interests and emerging commitments, and to experience directly the kind of value choices and conflicts involved in professional life. The link between theory and practice that is so often lost can be provided by seminars and assignments, coordinated with the internships, that involve values analysis, criticism, and consciousness. Such programs could invite professional practitioners to discuss the value issues that they face in their daily work. Students' research reports, logs, or journals can be structured around many of the characteristic questions of values education. With the right preparation and supervision, students find that their internships offer them an opportunity to confront real ethical and value issues, issues that otherwise are only abstractions.

Biography and Autobiography. Choice is no more concrete and revealing than in the lives of individual human beings. The record of a life can communicate the passion and significance of issues as lived, and reveal as well how various tests have been applied to measure success and failure, meaning and fulfillment.

Authenticity and consistency are two criteria of valuing that students can explore in a study of personal lives. Do persons act on the values they claim to hold, and are their values based on personal choice or external pressures? Memoirs also provide an excellent way to explore the issues of self-deception and self-justification. It would be worthwhile, for example, to review several of the Watergate memoirs, including Richard Nixon's, as examples of the way persons may lose their awareness of the moral meaning of their actions. Virtually all the Watergate memoirists discuss having succumbed to the error of self-deception. To read their works is to gain a deeper appreciation of the frailty of human moral consciousness and the temptations of self-deception.

Instructors' Roles and Responsibilities

The foregoing examples illustrate a wide variety of curricular possibilities in values education. They could be implemented as emphases within existing courses or as separate courses and programs. Although very diverse, they share a common set of premises. Rather than being organized mainly by the logic and structure of an academic discipline, these courses and programs derive their patterns and objectives from several sources. They consider first the nature of values and value choices, and then seek to address them by means of an appropriate subject matter. They use relevant disciplinary methods, but combine these with the tools of critical values inquiry. They show, in effect, that to teach values is to teach about values, to values, and for values.

In these proposed courses, certain teaching materials and methods are especially appropriate. Perhaps the dominant pedagogical characteristic is the need for a continuing movement between experience and reflection, the concrete and the abstract, practice and theory. Case studies and case histories, court decisions, policy statements, ethical codes, primary sources, and artistic works all provide the rich texture of experience as lived, from which values can be elicited and made the subject of critical and theoretical analysis. Discussions of cases in values education need to steer a course between aimless comments and lock-step responses. The broad goal should be to locate alternative possibilities and to consider their consequences, to see how value commitments shape the alternatives, and, as appropriate, to review the values themselves as to their consistency, coherence, comprehensiveness, adequacy, and duration.

Just as there are some topics and materials that seem especially suggestive for values education, so there are new roles and responsibilities for the instructor. The student's "equilibrium" has to be tolerantly and supportively challenged through imaginative discussions in which there is a genuine and demanding give-and-take between and among peers and instructor. An atmosphere of acceptance and openness has to prevail, as respect is accorded to the dignity of all participants, even when their positions are criticized. The instructor must communicate his or her faith in the students' ability to offer worthwhile responses to difficult problems. Effective teaching for values involves open-ended discussions and the occasional use of techniques such as role playing, debates, simulations, and games. These strategies and others are useful because students often find it difficult to take positions and defend them publicly. Students may feel more comfortable working in a group of four or five, with each group responsible for developing and defending a point of view. This arrangement allows students to shape and to argue their positions in a supportive setting that frees them from saying only what they think would please their professor. Role playing gives students the chance to try on positions without having to commit themselves seriously. Assuming the role of a notable historical or contemporary figure and arguing with an antagonist could be a memorable and worthwhile educational experience.

Good teaching also requires a willingness on the part of the instructor to shed the role of authority and at relevant times to reveal his or her own values and commitments, with all the risk and vulnerability that this entails. Robert T. Hall and John U. Davis characterize the need for candor in this way, "By being open and honest with his students, the teacher will help them to be open and honest about their thoughts and feelings with him and, in the process, with themselves and with one another. The best example a moral education teacher can give his students is his candor when formulating and expressing his own decisions" (1975, p. 117). At the same time, effective values education requires not less but more rigor and discipline by asking that objective critical standards be sought precisely within the passion and conflict of human experience. The instructor must serve as a model of self-criticism in the correction of personal biases and preferences. The entire process would fail miserably if students were pressed and challenged only to agree with the precise content of the professor's own value system. The surest guarantee against such indoctrination is for the instructor to help students develop their own skills in the analysis, consciousness, and criticism of values. In doing this effectively, the instructor affords the student access to the tools of autonomy and personal choice, the strongest protection against indoctrination.

We find once again that values education is able to unify approaches that usually exist in mutual hostility. Education is not therapy, and much of the talk about affective learning is intellectually thin. But good values teaching does rely on strong interpersonal skills because values education is more than the mastery of information and formal methods; it is the marriage of probing and rigorous intellectual analysis with empathy and human sensitivity. As Carl Rogers describes humanistic education, "Learning becomes life, and a very vital life at that. The student is on his way, sometimes excitedly, sometimes reluctantly, to becoming a learning, changing, being" (1969, p. 115).

Another required task in values education is one that is strangely missing in most of higher education. To be fully effective, values education depends on the instructor's accurate and sensitive reading of the students' cultural and developmental milieu. Instructors must establish a point of contact with the world of the students' experience. Instructors may have to make an explicit effort to interpret and decode the rapidly changing symbols and expressions of the cultural, psychological, and intellectual world of students. Developmental theorists like Erikson, Piaget, Kohlberg, W. Perry, and others have provided persuasive evidence regarding the moral and intellectual stages through which human beings pass. These stages provide a kind of filter that selects as reality certain features of experience. Limits are set as to what can even count as true, authoritative, good, or meaningful. Values educators who lack a sense of what these stages and filters are, of how students typically "see things," will miss their mark. Courses for freshmen should not be designed and taught in the same way as those for seniors. An effort aimed at teaching values can hardly hope to succeed if it ignores the very consciousness it hopes to affect.

Values Development

We argued earlier that the analysis, consciousness, and criticism of values can provide students a basis for changing their values. That there is such a possibility is highly significant, but it is also limited. There is no guarantee that values education can carry to term the process that it is able to initiate. Influences on human conduct are vastly complex and include strong cultural, psychological, and physiological forces. History, moreover, gives full and tragic testimony to the moral frailty of mankind, to the elaborate forms of human self-interest and evil. These realities can overpower value commitments or render them captive to alien and powerful drives—for power or status or security or whatever. Ultimately the self has dominion over values, so they follow all the self's adventures and misadventures. The self may experience the claims arising from a value but may choose not to respond or be unable to respond. It may at any time adopt other values or disvalues. The tie that values create between knowing and doing, and the link to change that values education provides, can be severed in the fissure between the self one is and the self that one might be. More than analytical and critical awareness is required for the full flowering of the self and its values.

The foregoing remarks suggest the limitations of education

to affect student values through the academic program alone. Yet there are other dimensions of the total educational experience in which the process of values development can and does take hold. To reach its full potential, values education will have to encompass the total life of the campus. Virtually every feature of collegiate life presents significant opportunities for fostering personal growth and for contributing to the development of a student's system of values. Values are formed and reformed precisely through human interaction, and the collegiate environment has a distinctive set of human relationships that can influence personal development.

Images of Campus Life. In order to situate the problems and possibilities for values development in collegiate life, it is helpful to sketch in broad outline the recent changes in the contours of the social and moral environment. During the past two decades, student rules and regulations in the social and moral realm have been reduced to a minimum, services have been multiplied many times over, and the students' formal role in college decision making has been established and codified. Two dominant images of the students' relationship to the institution have emerged or have been more sharply defined. As images, they tend to control assumptions, which in turn define policies. Students are increasingly pictured as consumers with preferences operating in a marketplace or as citizens with rights living in a special society. The older images of the student as a scholar with responsibilities in a community of scholars, or as a youth with duties in a large-scale family have not disappeared. Yet they have been moved aside, entering the mind's eye fitfully and providing a blurred and partial vision of what is happening on the campus.

Like all "parents" experiencing a change in roles, college administrations have both resented and enjoyed the students' growing rights and independence. They have been puzzled, but indulgent, while witnessing students' strident claims for autonomy accompanied by requests for more and more supportive services. Administrators have felt some genuine relief in being able to abandon ineffective and hypocritical regulations about everything from dress to chapel attendance. But they have also felt increasingly troubled as they have watched honor codes lose their force and have observed the growth of a corrosive privatism and an expedient competitiveness. In effect, most colleges have given up moralism without having a compelling morality to offer in its place. These changes in the campus environment have been wrought, of course, through the presence of certain new values—autonomy, tolerance, and personal freedom. But the counterveiling commitments—responsibility, community, and integrity—have not easily found new forms in which to come to expression.

Now is obviously not a time when the possibilities of a college or a university to become a compelling human and moral community seem particularly promising. Not all institutions have been affected by the foregoing trends in the same way, but all exist in the same environment and respond to the common elements in it. In all likelihood, the days are gone forever when a college or university could create a sanctuary by devising and enforcing a distinctive set of moral regulations. Many forces block this way for all but the tiniest handful of institutions. Federal and state laws and regulations on countless subjects now define much of the fabric of collegiate norms and relations. The consumer movement considers education like any other service: payment of a fee gives the purchaser the right to a series of specific services. Majority status at age eighteen and federal, contractual, and constitutional law have set a new juridical framework for a college's relationships with its students. Without doubt, these developments have helped to right serious wrongs and to correct an often arrogant sense of educational institutions as special preserves. And yet, without doubt, not by intent but by results, consumerism, contractualism, and federal activism have helped to deaden the spirit of community. These developments and others like them, such as vocationalism, define minimal standards of conduct and are designed to protect against abuse. They provide penalties for doing wrong, but cannot define or offer incentives for superior achievement. They build a floor but not a ceiling. They define procedures but not ultimate goals. This is particularly relevant, and painfully obvious, in a sphere of human self-actualization like education. Education at its best is characterized by a profound searching in the depths of human experience, at the edges of knowledge, and on the borders of the future. What the human enterprise itself has become and ever will be is tied intimately to what we can know, teach, and learn. For education to work as it must, all participants must feel a compelling sense of its importance, deep bonds of loyalty to the truth and to fellow truth seekers, and forms of intellectual and interpersonal commitment that dismiss minimal boundaries. Education is an open-ended and intense process leading where it will. Whatever portion of time, energy, and engagement is needed to reach the goal is what must be given. At its heart education is much like religion at its best—an everlasting quest for universal and enduring forms of meaning. If the consumer and the citizen are to participate fully, they must do so as learners and persons.

As these images of the student as consumer and as citizen have worked themselves into everyday campus life, they have narrowed the college's context and concern for values education. The explanation for this rests as much with the academy's reactions as it does with external forces. There is always just so much energy to give to one's responsibilities, and higher education has devoted large quantities to both real and imagined scuffles with government officials, insistent students, and the courts. The crucial problem is that minimal requirements have been mistaken for goals. The concern to satisfy regulations, to provide contractual services, and to stay out of court has displaced the intensity of the concern for the depth and quality of the students' total educational experience and for their growth as persons. While large measures of genuine commitment to students are still expressed by college instructors and staff members, at the same time, one senses that the relationship with students for many on the campus has narrowed. It has come to focus largely on pragmatic academic "outcomes" or on the services owed to a consumer. Faculty members, administrators, and staff responded in various ways to students' demands and militancy during the troubled late sixties and early seventies, but most faculty members withdrew, feeling that the fray was someone else's to fight. This disengagement marked the end of the official and historic role of the faculty in student life outside the classroom. If and when administrators recovered from the shell shock of those same years, their concerns were absorbed by budgets and new federal laws and regulations. In all, it is to a thin band of values, those lying in the sphere of social and academic contracts, that most faculty and staff members feel they should address themselves. It appears that the concern for the student as a whole person always belongs somewhere else.

Again, the campus has turned away from meddling and moralizing, but has not found credible and effective ways to meet its expressed commitment to its students as persons. Some of these trends can best be measured through changes in the tone and quality of expectations for student conduct and achievement. Many commentators have suggested that an alive and demanding sense of expectancy throughout the campus can powerfully shape students' values. (See, in particular, Eddy, 1959, chap. 2.) As institutional goals have split and narrowed, this sense of expectancy has lost its focus and much of its force. Increasingly, colleges' goals are being set by external sources, whether they be government agencies or professional societies; the unity and clarity of the colleges' expectation of student performance and conduct are thereby fractured. We are often all too ready to accept and reward imprecise, shoddy, and falsified work, because we are not sure what to expect, when, and of whom. We are facing a generation of students who are less skilled and more pragmatic than their predecessors, and we are unprepared for it. We are uncertain about who our students really are and what motivates them.

Personal Relationships and Expectations. These recent developments in college life provide a difficult setting in which to pursue, extend, and deepen the educational task of the analysis, awareness, and criticism of values. Values press claims that go beyond the minimal and the contractual, that require a depth of self-questioning into which the student as a consumer might prefer not to enter. Yet the collegiate environment, especially in the smaller institutions, continues to provide an unusual opportunity to foster intellectual, moral, personal, and religious values. If such an environment did not exist, it would be worth creating. The research of William Perry, Douglas Heath, Arthur Chickering, Howard R. Bowen, and Alexander Astin clearly shows this. Colleges and universities, especially if they are residential, offer programs and services and afford relationships that encompass most of a student's waking experience during the course of four pivotal years. A community of this kind should be able, if it chooses, to provide distinctive and effective possibilities for the growth of human persons. We are convinced, to be more specific, that the nature and quality of human relationships on a campus provides a primary and profound resource for influencing the values of students. There is nothing surprising in this, of course, because values arise precisely in the relationship between the self, its companions, and the physical world. The many dimensions and expressions of reciprocal expectation between persons—of care and mutual reliance, of challenge and affirmation—are deeply formative of human values.

In a small college especially, the sense of expectancy can be rooted in a relationship with students as persons, and thereby related to basic values. Without forcing its proper bounds and distinctive purposes, the relationship between instructors and students, for example, can include active and mutual respect and accountability. Students and faculty members can feel that what one does or fails to do matters to another person and is part of a common enterprise. They acknowledge one another's efforts in the context of shared human care and concern. A student's ideas and changing views matter to the instructor as *that* student's ideas. What the student says during the eighth week of class is noted and compared with his or her position during the second. Each student feels part of an important undertaking, one that is shared with the instructor. Esther Raushenbush claims that what students cherish above all else is this sense of a shared experience, "They [the students] know the teacher is going through something when the students are; the students speak of this when it is happening, and often afterward, for the sense of communion lasts. Such teachers care about what becomes of their students, but their concern for their students is not limited by a wish to do something *for* them. There is important experience to be discovered, work to be done, a world to function in; and the education of the students, their growth to manhood, the personal enlargement education should bring, has a better chance of accomplishment if the teacher can forward the experience, reveal the work to do, help them to find in study ways to function" (1964, p. 135).

Relationships of the kind described here do not require friendship and closeness. That is not the point. Rather, they depend upon a shared set of values, from which spring both mutual confirmation and judgment. The aim is not to invade the self's privacy; rather, it is to address those common commitments, promises, and values, such as truth and excellence, through which persons become enfranchised to participate in a community of liberal learning.

In such a relationship among persons, values like honesty, integrity, and responsibility exercise their full and proper force. If all participants do not share the expectation that values such as these are personal requirements as well as institutional forms, the entire academic enterprise becomes a cynical or a routine process. Plagiarism, cheating, and deception in all its expressions, do not merely violate the codes in a handbook, they destroy the interpersonal integrity of a community. If students have become cavalier about personal honesty, one of the reasons is that they have not encountered a uniform and demanding sense of expectancy regarding the meaning of personal integrity. As Edward D. Eddy comments in quoting a student remark, "The student who admits to cheating will admit as readily to specific instances in which he would not consider the act because of the attitude of a particular professor. 'That man . . . expects so much of himself and of me that I would never let him down. If I did let him down, I'd go down, too' " (1959, p. 12).

Many of the perspectives we are suggesting can be summed up in the idea of the teacher as model or mentor. One learns best the values required for good scholarship—patience, tolerance, rigor, fairness, precision—by seeing them in action, by experiencing their authority with and through another person. But we would like to emphasize another potential feature of the relationship, the claim that the self experiences to strive for its own fulfillment, to reach its utmost possibilities. Teachers, and others, can effectively require students to face themselves, to become responsible for their own learning, to take themselves seriously as independent thinkers and agents, and to unearth the best that is in them. The self-discipline and skill required to draw the very best out of students, setting them free to encounter themselves all the while, are considerable. Instructors must engage students as persons, and send them back again and again to wrestle with their choices and their values—with themselves. It depends, finally, on the instructor's own high expectations of his or her own teaching, on the effort always to improve and to revise the next lecture, to clarify again that obscure point, to listen, really to listen, to what students are saying, and to show why the topic at hand matters.

If, as we suggest, values can be most decisively affected through personal relationships and expectations, through challenge and acceptance, then other aspects of the campus environment become significant. We have no reason to expect students to grow as persons—in understanding, tolerance, compassion, honesty, fairness, and responsibility—unless these are the reigning values in the total conduct of campus life. By what norms, in the name of what values, do we carry out our various duties and participate in the common life of the institution? How do we as faculty and staff members and students really treat one another? In our relationships, we always have mutual expectations. We must examine these and ask ourselves probing questions about them. Do we meet institutional adversity with self-pity or with courage? Are rumors challenged, or do they run free? Do we seek answers for the questions we have, or do we invent our own? Do we insist on mutual respect, or are we satisfied with suspicion? Do we criticize in order to build, or to destroy? Are we willing to help those in need, or can we always find good excuses not to do so? Do our acts as an institution contribute to the common good, or do we claim that we have no social responsibilities? We seldom see concerns of this kind classed with professional ethics. A strong case should be made, however, for including the human quality of organizational life within our sense of professional responsibility. When the effort is made to develop a code of campus rights and responsibilities, these basic qualities of relationship should not be neglected but placed at the heart of the deliberations. It seems clear that the general tone of campus life has a vivid impact on student values and conduct, for it provides the context and sets the expectations for their relationships with one another and with us. Colleges and universities teach values by their very being and by their structures, and this influence should not be neglected in values education.

Woodrow Wilson's comment that "a college is not only a body of studies but a mode of association" summarizes the ideas that have been presented here. The image that we propose for the student in this "mode of association" is neither that of the consumer, nor that of the citizen, although these elements are included. Rather, the image of the student as a person in a scholarly community should define our understanding of the possibilities for values education in collegiate life. The terms *person* and *community* are correlative. A community is a person writ large, especially in terms of values. Values, as standards, are precisely those bonds of relationship through which persons become good to and for one another. In finding the values in my community, I find myself; and in finding myself, I find the community.

We can understand, then, why in a genuine community there is such a strong sense of mutual responsibility and such force of judgment when a norm has been broken. When persons take upon themselves and into their own identities the values of a community, they have *become* those values. The characteristic sense of loss of self, with its pressures of conscience, arises when a value is violated. Only now there is not just a generalized sense that one has failed oneself and mankind at large, there is a sharp sense of having let down precisely these real persons, these companions in community. As one of the students in Heath's studies put it in discussing the college honor code, " 'It forced me to realize what I do, well . . . ultimately what I do, I do not only for or against myself, which is half of it; the other half is for or against the community' " (1968, p. 210).

We find, yet again, that the theme of values offers an integrative approach—in this case between student life and student learning. The repeated disappointment of many faculty members that the curriculum is all in pieces is echoed in the forlorn complaint of sensitive student affairs officers that student life is fragmented. It is split between learning and living, between the classroom and the dorm, between work and fun. The academic community's concern for values can provide a strong thread of continuity. The very values that are at the heart of the academic enterprise—truth seeking and truth telling, tolerance for divergent views, responsibility to one's peers—are incomprehensible outside of a human community to sustain them. Whatever else, the college or the university as a scholarly community has the responsibility to develop a lively awareness and a deepened commitment to the very values for which it stands.

Strategies for Values Development

The formation of a campus environment that affects and fosters values and personal growth is obviously no simple task. As we have seen, many of the forces that influence the campus are beyond its control. Then, too, like all organizations, colleges and universities are victim to inertia; they easily succumb to established patterns and routines when setting priorities and allocating scarce resources. Professional identities, too, often find a comfortable investment in the familiar. Giving uninspired lectures on the known may seem preferable to the possible chaos that might result from a bold venture into the unknown—especially when one has no time to plan it. Finally, administrative life in mass higher education has become predominantly managerial, paralleling the disciplinary specialities of the curriculum. Like their classroom colleagues, contemporary administrators are functional specialists. The past decade has produced a parade of new administrative systems and procedures, most of which have made the administration of higher education ever more like the management of any corporation or nonprofit organization. Student and management information systems, planning and budgeting procedures, personnel systems, management by objectives, marketing systems, organizational and staff development techniques—all define the world of the contemporary college administrator. Once again, values education's best possibilities initially seem thwarted—in this case by the administrative need to simply keep the institution running.

Any effective strategy for values education must take account of these realities, and seek to turn them to its own advantage. Educators must first acquire a full and sharp awareness of values and their educational possibilities. A lively sense of organizational and educational theory, of human values and human development, can yield new ways of seeing the campus. Since the world is not likely to change nor administrative and organizational complexity to abate, the pivotal point in creating a potent campus environment for values education is critical awareness. From awareness will flow insight into specific strategies, tactics, and actions. If values development is to be effective, it must become the constant touchstone for the administrative system itself. We cannot romantically seek to escape the system, but in every way try to transform it. In doing so, administrators may find their way back to the humanizing possibilities of their roles as educators.

In exploring several strategies for values development, we will not offer a systematic survey nor detail specific programs or activities, except for purposes of illustration. There is a limit to how much guidance the experience of one institution can have for another as norms and practices have a definite history and are not readily transferable from one college to another. On a more general level, though, a number of broad strategies suggest themselves.

Awareness. Many colleges and universities have elaborate information systems with which to track enrollment, grading patterns, retention rates, and similar measures of student performance and choice. Increasingly, too, systems have been developed to provide all sorts of marketing data to assist in student recruitment. Far less often available, however, is information on the informal norms of the institution as a human community, on the expectations that operate on a daily, human level between faculty members and students, students and students, faculty and administration, and others. What, in other words, are the forms of behavior that are ignored, tolerated, praised, and blamed? What are the penalties for breaking the norms? What *does* the senior tell the freshman? How hard must one work, or appear to work, or say one works? Is preparation for graduate and professional school the silent requirement for academic respectability? Is it all right for a faculty member to praise an administrator, and for an administrator not to be resentful or cynical about the faculty? An examination of these psychological and social attitudes is the point of entry and of expression for an analysis of underlying values. One can scarcely take any steps to improve an environment unless one knows something of its distinctive problems and opportunities. Perhaps a new mechanism is needed to convey information, or a different decision-making body to handle built-up frustrations.

Educational institutions need a continuing, carefully planned audit of how people understand their own roles and responsibilities and those of others in the community.

The information one acquires about the informal norms and values of the community can then be interpreted in the context of theories of psychological, moral, and values development. Within the past two decades a number of significant and useful theories about the stages of human development have emerged and, as we have seen, a number of these have been applied to college students. Theorists offer a set of rich insights that educators can apply to some of the characteristic problems and aspirations of young adults. (For a summary of seven developmental theorists' work and their relevance to student services, see Knefelkemp, Widick, and Parker, 1978.) It is not unreasonable to expect that faculty members and administrators would benefit significantly from becoming competent interpreters of these materials. Developmental theory can provide at least some common point of reference, if not agreement, in the intellectual world at large, which provides virtually no shared vision of human excellence. Developmental theory can offer an orientation for action, for interpreting conduct, and for devising programs to respond coherently to campus problems and opportunities. A rash of campus destruction may signal a need not just for more security but for dorm programs on handling emotions. Or, a proposed curricular program for freshmen on value issues may be rejected in favor of one for juniors or seniors, whom developmental theorists suggest are much surer of their own values.

A consciousness of actual campus norms and values, perhaps interpreted with the aid of developmental theories, provides an excellent base for a realistic statement of an institution's objectives in the realm of values. They should not sit on a shelf, but be communicated widely and wisely. A set of conscious objectives seems essential lest one not be able to tell whether what is the case should be the case, and whether specific activities are having their intended effect. The objectives function as a kind of easily amendable constitution, aiding members of the community to organize energy for present tasks, to focus insight for the future, and to provide understanding of the past.

Since most colleges and universities are periodically engaged in formal long-range planning, the effort to state institutional mission and objectives in terms of values has a natural administrative home. The typical planning effort, however, is usually preoccupied with fiscal projections or questions of organizational structure. The development of students' values through education is usually either expressed in platitudes or forgotten. Once administrators and faculty members become aware of the institution's responsibility, they should have little difficulty in keeping questions of institutional values tied closely to the formal procedures of planning.

Organizational, Faculty, and Staff Development. Higher education is just beginning to give serious attention to the important devices of organizational, faculty, and staff development. This long-neglected area has been an essential and regular part of organizational effectiveness in most other types of institutions. Through programs of all sorts, faculty members and staff professionals can be helped to understand more fully the needs and motivations of students and, not incidentally, their own as well. They can develop skills to handle conflicts effectively and to reconceive and restructure organizational roles and responsibilities. Out of such programs emerge all kinds of specific objectives and projects, ranging from student activities to new organizations for campus decision making. For example, rather than continuing to deplore the weaknesses in campus advising, effort could and should be directed toward training interested individuals in basic counseling and listening skills, as well as in some of the developmental dynamics of young adults. Obviously any efforts of this kind have to be based on careful planning that includes those who are to be involved. Poor preparation or the wrong match of personalities would essentially kill a promising program for the duration of the longest memory on campus.

The community of scholars can and should practice with much more frequency its own skills on itself. The nature of organizational life, developments in higher education, curricular trends, institutional responsibilities, and so forth are increasingly important areas of knowledge. Consider, for example, the possibilities of a formal seminar of faculty members and administrators on the topic suggested above—personal and moral development during the college years. It would be hard for any group of educators not to be affected by a careful study of the work of W. Perry, Heath, or Chickering, and many others. Their research has so many implications for the way one teaches and relates to students that the eventual practical results could be very impressive indeed.

Participation in the Life of the Organization. College life takes place in a number of physical, social, and academic settings, ranging from the classroom to the snack bar. These are all appreciated in theory as providing important opportunities for education and growth, but reality falls far short of the ideal. Students come and go, spirit rises and falls, and there seems little one can do to change the trends. The educational opportunities that are present, though, should give one pause. The ability to understand how an organization really works and to contribute to its effectiveness are pivotal achievements.

The opportunity to shape campus regulations and to feel a responsibility for them, to run an organization, or to serve on a college-wide committee are value-laden experiences. They are important aspects of education. To understand human motivation in action, to experience firsthand the constraint of a budget, the disinterest and foibles of friends, the criticism of foes, and still to make a personal difference, are priceless lessons. They contribute to the self-understanding and self-esteem that values education fosters and on which it depends.

The lost educational opportunities in these kinds of involvements can be illustrated by the peculiar fate of student involvement in college governance. The hard-won rights of the 1960s became the forsaken duties of the 1970s. On either side of the decade are assumptions that need to be challenged by values education. On the one hand, there is the romantic illusion that change comes by a morally righteous snap of the fingers and, on the other, the disregard for any change that does not affect the private self. What education has missed, often by neglecting simple strategies, is the chance to show students how human organizations function. As one prime example, students on committees have rarely been oriented to the task at hand, given a thorough background on the issues, held to standards of accountability by their peers or anyone else, and asked to provide an evaluation of their experience. Learning to work through an organizational chain would heighten students' self-awareness and personal effectiveness. This one example has analogues throughout the campus, in student activities, clubs, athletics, and dormitories. Student affairs personnel clearly have a primary educational role in all these contexts, but one that too often is lost under piles of regulations, budget sheets, and memos.

Selection and Evaluation of Faculty and Staff. We have suggested that personal and institutional relationships and expectations are prime movers in the realm of values. An institution's personnel system and procedures are thus centrally important in contributing to values education. The selection of people who truly care about students and what happens to them, whose professional aims and recognition are not solely drawn from outside the institution, is necessary if values development is to take place. In effective values education, faculty and staff members find their fulfillment in the fulfillment of others—their students.

A critical awareness of values can be easily and decisively related to an existing personnel review system. Colleges that use the basic approach of management by objectives can make the development of values a conscious objective that will shape specific goals and provide a criterion for viewing program accomplishments and problems. Once principal administrators inject a concern for values development into the process of personnel evaluations, that concern will work its way into the continuing daily activities of the administration.

The Practice of Tradition. Values are always embodied in realized forms of human presence. They can be brought to consciousness and strengthened through the practice of a community's traditions. All communities rehearse and foster their identities through events, celebrations, and memories of one kind or another, and the college or university is no exception. A community such as a college that practices reflective criticism can be expected to test and correct its remembrances but it cannot do without them. Memory and ritual combine to express the community's meaning to itself. If it prizes good scholarship, it makes sense to reward it; if it has a foundational faith, it is good to celebrate it; if it is proud of its past, it is best to honor it. What a place stands for can be communicated in these moments as a valuable point of repair in a confusing and fragmented world.

The effort to build a reflective educational community of persons is not a simple process of rational calculation. In many ways the experience of human community is as much a gift as it is an achievement. The chances of success can be heightened, though, by a consciousness of values based on at least a basic grasp of themes in human and values development. As with all other institutions, colleges and universities teach values by their very existence. Their policies tend toward fairness or unfairness, their standards toward consistency or inconsistency, their choices toward justice or injustice. The problem is not to invent programs, activities, and contexts through which values might be influenced. These already exist in abundance. The task, rather, is to convert whatever must happen and does happen into an occasion, however modest, for the full flowering of human possibility.

Six

Impact on Academic, Political, and Religious Choices

→»→»→»→»→»→»‹‹‹‹‹‹‹‹‹‹‹‹‹‹‹

Most contemporary statements of the goals of liberal education and professional education refer to the development of a student's sense of moral and civic responsibility. Reviewing the practice of contemporary education, however, one finds very few clear indications of how these ends actually are served. In the previous chapters, we have described a set of educational emphases through which the domain of values, as appropriately understood, can be explored in ways consistent with the university's methods and responsibilities. Our approach to values education accentuates, intensifies, and reorders methods of critical inquiry that have a long tradition in higher learning. It does not invent new ones.

We present values education as involving a plurality of possible subject matters, not limited to the theory of values or the study of ethics, although these are central. We emphasize certain teaching strategies and materials because they are appropriate to the way values function, not for the sake of innovation in itself. We give a major educational role to the campus as a community of persons that can enlarge and deepen the classroom experience. In all, we have described values education as one of the central themes and methods in liberal education and as an important one in professional education. Just as, for example, one could successfully argue that the ability to communicate effectively is one of the goals of education, so one can say that competency in the sphere of values analysis, consciousness, and criticism is another. Just as the development of good communication skills requires both specific courses and general emphases throughout the academic program, so, too, does a mature understanding of values depend on a variety of curricular and extracurricular experiences.

If these are the contours of values and education, what are its limits and its possibilities? Having described the process, what can we now say about the content of values education? To what is a college or a university—its faculty, staff, and students—committing itself if it makes values education a goal and accepts it as a responsibility? What can it expect to accomplish and in what areas? Will the basic intellectual values receive exclusive attention, or will moral values receive serious notice as well? Should personal goals and values come under scrutiny in the collegiate setting, and how should social and political commitments be approached? What is the place of religious values, especially in the nonsectarian and public institutions?

Adequate answers to these queries depend upon honest and detailed answers to a prior question, What kind of college or university do we want ours to be? Not every institution can nourish every worthy value. In the realm of values there are no multiuniversities. Choices have to be made, especially as to the specific forms in which values are implemented. Within all the real diversity, however, are also broad parallels in the kinds of values that educational institutions in this society can develop. Let us explore the three basic areas of academic, democratic, and ultimate values.

We shall do so by summarizing much of our earlier discussion and by tacitly applying to these clusters of values the five procedures that have been discussed—values analysis, consciousness, criticism, pedagogy, and development. Now that all five tools are at hand, we can put them to work on different sets of actual values.

Academic Values

As we have seen on several occasions, especially in discussing the morality of scholarship, a number of ironies persist in the standard academic attitude toward values. The effort to eschew all judgments based on preferences and unsubstantiated opinion (commonly called *value judgments*) has tended to blind us to the values, the standards, to which all the disciplines are committed. Values are inevitably and universally present in all human experiences as the standards of human choice; they necessarily guide even the pursuit of the most quantified and specialized knowledge. They are present as the inescapable conditions of meaningful human thought. The values in question are not specific value judgments; they are normative intellectual and moral patterns of intention and choice. Intellectual values include precision, rigor, clarity, consistency, and truth; moral values include honesty, tolerance, respect, and self-criticism. Intellectual work could not be what it is without certain values that reside as structures in personal intention and activity. Douglas Heath convincingly describes the nexus between moral and intellectual development: "Finally, and more compelling, maturing of certain values is so intrinsically a part of intellectual development that the failure to develop one limits the growth of the other. Intellectual activity requires honesty, objectivity, openness to alternatives, flexibility, humility, respect for dissenting views, and so on. Associated with intellectual activity is an ethic about what is appropriate intellectual activity. A person who fabricates or distorts information, consciously ignores contradictory data, plagiarizes the work of others, and interprets information to fit some purpose other than truth loses the trust and respect of others. A liberal education must educate for the ethic of truth if it is not to produce intellectual psychopaths" (1968, pp. 259–260).

Colleges and universities thus have an undeniable responsibility for actively developing their students' academic values. Any self-understanding of their role that neglects this obligation would deeply falsify their historic sense of themselves. To disregard the link between values and intellectual work would make the entire enterprise of education unintelligible. Truth makes imperious and universal demands, especially on those who claim to be its special servants. Those who plead that all values are relative make little sense.

What, then, can be done by colleges and universities to foster the development of these essential moral and intellectual values and virtues? Should faculty members offer pontifical lectures on truth and goodness, and administrators enact new sets of sharp-eyed regulations? From all that we have seen about the nature of values and human agency, effective values education does not consist of inculcating abstract truths. We are drawn back to a series of emphases that reside in the actions and relationships of individual human beings. There is the home of values. Programs and practices can and should be shaped to carry forward and institutionalize these individual responsibilities, but they can never replace them. We see more clearly now why the concern for the campus as a community cannot be an administrative or rhetorical afterthought. It provides the context for relationships that either foster or impede the development of the values that are central to the very purposes of the institution. Relationships among members of the community—among faculty members, between faculty members and students, staff members and students, students with one another, and so on—determine the depth to which individuals make genuine personal commitments to the academic virtues. Honor codes can nourish and express these commitments, but cannot create them *ex nihilo*. Scholarship depends on these virtues but is not able in itself to reveal their wider and compelling meaning. The development of students' values requires that the academic community practice an analytical and critical consciousness of academic values in a wide variety of tacit and explicit ways. It will appear in statements of institutional objectives, in systematic classroom discussions about academic honesty, in statements of rights and responsibilities, in curricular programs and emphases, in personal models of scholarly objectivity, in the language of the president and the deans, in orientation programs and workshops, and in other appropriate formal or informal settings. When our critical awareness of values comes into play, we never find an absence of values. Truth or expediency, excellence or mediocrity, self-criticism or self-indulgence—these shape the academic life. The specific capability of the academic community's critical awareness is to raise insistent, telling questions about its faithfulness to itself. Through such awareness, a community can initiate a continuing transformation in the expectations, commitments, and values of its common life.

It is easy to think that intellectual values such as truth and honesty are somehow guaranteed in the regular practice of scholarship and research. But a precariousness, a human fragility, bedevils the implementation of even such universal values as truth telling and truth seeking. One's submission to these values involves a choice—for truth rather than some other value or convenience, perhaps one that might even bring fame or fortune. A difficult choice is involved in accepting results that disprove one's hard-won theories, or in delaying or qualifying attractive claims that the evidence just does not support. Perhaps introductory courses in philosophy and natural science, and every freshmen orientation program, should find a place for study of a work like Watson's *The Double Helix* (1968). This account of Watson and Crick's discovery of DNA reveals the extraordinary temptations, competitiveness, and human ambition surrounding one of the crucial scientific discoveries of the century. For students to learn that truth has a high cost, but that it is pre-eminently worth it, can be a triumphant achievement of values education. The love of truth is no mean virtue.

Democratic Values

Higher education and our society currently are marked deeply by the pursuit of fulfillment in strictly private terms. Education is viewed as the intense concentration on individual and marketable skills, and life as a perpetual stream of self-improvement projects. Tom Wolfe calls it the *me decade*, and Christopher Lasch terms it the *culture of narcissism*. This preoccupation with self stands in sharp contrast with the historic role of education as the preparation for public life and responsibility in a democracy. What we broadly can call the civic role of education continues to stand as a self-professed goal, but little civic consciousness or content appears in the actual practice of higher education. For many, an effort to foster a commitment to democratic values seems to involve an indoctrinative stance or old-fashioned piety. Institutions, however, are much like individuals. They cannot and do not maintain a perpetual neutrality in the realm of basic values. Even if that were desirable, it is simply not possible. In carrying out their purposes, all colleges and universities necessarily posit an implicit, but operative, view of human limits and possibilities that expresses itself in a set of values. Existence as an educational institution, or as a person, in a democratic society—a choice that we all have made or accepted—carries with it requisite moral, intellectual, and personal conditions. These conditions may not be universal, for other ways of life are possible, but they are the given values that serve as our lived requirements. They are reflected in a web of legal, professional, and personal obligations. If we were without these, we could not be what we are.

There is, then, a core of values that higher education in a pluralistic democracy must recognize and foster. These are not simply the procedural values of majority rule and self-governance, but the assumptions about human rights and dignity that stand behind the procedures. The U.S. Constitution, Bill of Rights, Declaration of Independence, and similar documents throughout the world, bespeak them and rely on them. Therefore, in addition to truth, strengthened commitments to tolerance, equality, respect for self and others, integrity, freedom, justice, and compassion assuredly are worthy goals of any education. These are among the primary conditions for cooperative life among persons in a democracy. They are the demands of civilized life in our time and place, and their development and practice are of enduring importance.

What can an institution of higher education do to foster these civic and democratic values? To envisage July Fourth oratory flooding the campus would be to misconceive the way values actually exist. Martin Buber offers a convincing illustration of how moralizing fails to reach its goals, "if I am concerned with the education of character, everything becomes problematic. I try to explain to my pupils that envy is despicable, and at once I feel the secret resistance of those who are poorer than their comrades. I try to explain that it is wicked to bully the weak, and at once I see a suppressed smile on the lips of the strong. I try to explain that lying destroys life, and something frightful happens: the worst habitual liar of the class produces a brilliant essay on the destructive power of lying. I have made the fatal mistake of giving instruction in ethics, and what I said is accepted as current coin of knowledge; nothing of it is transformed into character-building substance" (1955, p. 105).

Because values are inescapably present in historical and social circumstances, they do not have to be taught through exhortation. They are already in the situation that is at hand or under study; to teach values is to trace implications, elicit possibilities, and find directions. In many ways, to teach values basically means to address them, to attend to their presence. They are not taught simply by arguing for equality or freedom or justice as abstract principles. One traces their uncertain but real presence in significant historical moments, eliciting the checkered history of justice, for instance, in legal cases and legislative history, and finding the directions of freedom in instances of human conflict and triumph. As we discussed earlier, courses that focus on issues in public policy or social choice can be especially effective in revealing value conflicts and decisions. Once students have detected the pertinent values, they can use a critical apparatus to assess them. Ultimately, each student must question the adequacy, consistency, coherence, duration, and comprehensiveness of the relevant law, decision, or institution and find why and where others have stood and where he or she might take a stand. When pursued effectively, values education makes this kind of critical inquiry second-nature and ties it intimately to the self's own sense of itself. Conscience is then at work, testing self-gratification against social responsibility, racism against equality and dignity, self-righteousness against tolerance, and injustice against justice. Competing value claims are rarely unequivocal, but the democratic virtues persistently press toward policies and actions that result in a more open, harmonious, humane, and creative future. In large measure, one's values change through their own weight, by means of the confrontation between human consciousness and the possibilities of existence. There is a place in values education for abstract argument, and even for exhortation, but only when linked to the actualities of human sensibility and decision.

In the education of the civic self, the role of the college as a human community once again comes to the fore. One learns best how to participate responsibly in democratic institutions through practice, by doing so. College life offers the opportunity for the values of democratic participation and responsibility to be fostered and tested. A democracy fails without an active, alive citizenry; the same is largely true of a college or a university. There are academic spheres of expertise where majority rule does not apply, but the regular rounds of campus life in dormitories, dining halls, playing fields, classrooms, and meeting places provides the opportunity for a large measure of student self-governance. In taking responsibility and making decisions, students learn the ways of democracy in practice and how it works through accommodation and concilia- tion. All the rights, privileges, and values of democracy soon weaken without a prior sense of responsibility to be caringly in- volved in one's smaller and larger communities.

Current social and political trends have created a new urgency regarding the education of the civic self. The problems of the future in this and other societies are so complex and crucial that it is clear that values are no longer the icing on the educational cake. They may prove to be the whole cake. As we face ever de- clining natural resources and constantly rising human needs and expectations, the old rhetoric about "educating for democracy" suddenly has taken on genuine meaning. More than anything else, the future effectiveness of our democracy will depend upon edu- cated persons. The new ideal of education, however, will have to go far beyond the accumulation of knowledge and intellectual skills. It will focus upon a person's gaining the insight, responsibility, sensi- tivity, and courage to respond to change through intelligent choices. Higher education's contribution to society's well-being will be measured increasingly by its capacity to develop the powers and skills of decision making—as well as of knowing. Its success will depend on the soundness of the values which it can help to foster.

Out of education's responsibility for values will emerge new opportunities for solving human problems and meeting human needs.

Ultimate Values

At several points in our discussion, we have come upon what might be called the limits of values. We have seen how values are unable to prohibit a dominant destructive drive of a community or a person for its own greater power and glory. Values reveal the costs of human evil, but cannot control evil at its source. We also have discussed different forms of the relativity of values. At this point, we must consider some of the implications of the precariousness and limitations of values for higher education.

The problem of the relativism of values appears in its final and most difficult form at a level that we have not yet explored. For, finally, all values have their worth in terms of some underlying assumptions regarding human possibilities and their fulfillment. We find the premises for value systems in basic visions of human nature and destiny. Different images of the human condition yield fundamentally different values in which fulfillment is sought. Values are always *for* and *from* a central point of reference.

Eastern philosophies and religions, for example, propose a fundamental vision of life that contrasts sharply with that of our own culture. In these perspectives, human beings are viewed as *not-selves* who can escape the futility and transience of individualism only through disciplines and values that deny materiality. Even positions that share a similar world vision can disagree at critical and fundamental points. How best are we to conceive and develop our own individuality: as beings of matter or of reason, as rugged and solitary individuals or as persons in a community, as members or as functions of some definitive group? Toward what ultimate end are we tending: the classless society, the Kingdom of God, or a scientific utopia? Much of the political and economic tension that characterizes our lives can be traced to the conflicting value systems that arise from different points of departure and destiny.

Any college or university that chooses to encourage the development of values will have to face the hard challenge of this form of the relativity of values. As institutions engaged in the study of world cultures, they should not become strident partisans of "our way of life," nor doctrinaire concerning one of the many theories of human nature. At the same time, their effort to foster values cannot await a hypothetical synthesis of all possible visions of human life. The solution to the problem of relativism at this fundamental level comes through informed choice, not theory. In setting and implementing their educational goals, colleges and universities necessarily postulate, even if unconsciously, one among many possible visions of human good by positing a system of academic values, by asserting a kind of human faith in reason, truth, and intelligibility. Values education suggests that the selection of these premises be made critically and analytically, that differences among premises can be discussed and reasons offered in defense of one's commitments. Consider the possibility of exchanges between a behaviorist and a rationalist, a capitalist and a Marxist, or a Christian and a Buddhist. These discussions have their logical limits, but even the limits can be located and analyzed in terms of the criteria of valuing. Participants in such discussions would probably not understand or apply the criteria in the same way, and their disagreements could not be settled rationally. Yet it is important for students and educators to locate these final points at which a conversion to an entire other perspective seems the only way to resolve differences. Since all individuals make or accept commitments to a center or starting point for human values—a point with reference to which good is known to be good—there would seem to be no valid educational reasons to stop the process of values education short of these ultimate perspectives. The prosecution of the argument to this level rarely occurs, however, due to a confused understanding of the requirements of academic neutrality.

Some of these same issues can be revealed in a different light by considering the questions that arise around the starting point of a human value system. What gives worth to the center of worth itself? Where does the foundation find its own foundation? If we say, for example, that the human person in community is the center of the system, we find that the center itself is vulnerable and limited. As finite, it is anxious about its own security and meaning.

Persons face transience, suffering, constant threats to their own sense of esteem, and death. In other words, the meaning that values give is circumscribed, they "judge our way of being in the world, without finally judging the original act by which the subject becomes present to the world" (Mehl, 1957, p. 266, my translation). Although values offer meanings *in* existence, they cannot give the meaning *of* existence.

Yet we know that persons do not live without meaning, for they are so constituted as to require it. As H. Richard Niebuhr puts it, "the faith that life is worth living and the definite reference of life's meaning to specific beings or values is as inescapable a part of human existence as the activity of reason. . . . Without such faith men might exist, but not as selves. Being selves they as surely have something for which to live as selves as being rational they have objects to understand" (1939, p. 4). These choices involved in referring life's meaning to "specific beings or values" seem clear enough in ordinary experience. Certain things and realities—the self, status, democracy, the nation, wealth, success, truth, the family, or God—become the causes for which one literally lives. The cause as the object of faith comes to play a dual function in giving the self both a sense of fundamental self-esteem and a purpose for living. This cause, or many causes together, makes life worth living by providing the self with that in which it can trust for its own value and that to which it can be actively loyal in service in the wider world. In this sense, faith as an ultimate value appears as a given structure in all of human existence.

This analysis of the self's ultimate value commitments arises naturally out of the methods of values education. The apparatus of critical values inquiry can be applied to the objects of human faith. Not to do so, in fact, is to terminate arbitrarily the scope of the questions it poses. We can assess the adequacy, comprehensiveness, duration, consistency, and authenticity of our objects of faith. Do they give meaning for a time and then pass away, or do they endure? Do they establish wide or narrow circles of loyalty, solve or create conflicts in human relationships? Do they foster unity or division within the self? In sum, can they so dominate the negative factors of human experience and so foster the sense of the self's worth that they are fully adequate objects of faith? Is the subject of faith both ultimately powerful and universally good? (For a discussion of the criteria of diety, see Niebuhr, 1941, chap. 4.)

In pursuing the issue of ultimate values, we are analyzing questions that many would classify as religious. That is an understandable and even acceptable interpretation, but we need not necessarily use that term. It is more accurate to say that we are exploring the universal human phenomenon of faith as a value, faith as an experience of the meaning of life, that life is worth living. In doing so, we illustrate a way in which values education can address the age-old question of what constitutes the good life. Students ask themselves constantly, and often fervently about the kind of life they want to live or should live, about the kind of person they can be or should be, about what they should do with their lives. Vocational interests answer the query on one level, but their questions press for a deeper reply. Only rarely does the formal instructional program offer a disciplined set of procedures even to begin to speak to these issues. As we have noted, serious discussions of the topic of the good life have all but disappeared from contemporary philosophy. Values analysis, criticism, and consciousness offer methods to pursue these matters seriously and rigorously. The forms of inquiry are fully consistent with the appropriate rational methods of higher education, even in public and secular institutions. In fact, not to pursue value inquiry to this level is an artificial interruption of the process. The methods of critical values awareness speak directly to real and stirring human questions that have an ancient, respected lineage. If appropriately understood and internalized, they offer a means to guide a person through a lifetime of structured awareness and reflection about life's meaning and possibilities. Throughout the process, the freedom and responsibility of the individual to choose his or her own ultimate values is never in doubt. Values inquiry is neutral in its approach, while committed to the importance of studying values. Individual students and faculty members undoubtedly will find themselves arguing directly or indirectly for or against particular ends of life—personal achievement, the life of the mind, material success, faith in God, the classless society, or Nirvana. To be sure, not every object of devotion is able or will be seen as able to pass the tests of values inquiry. Personal choice in these issues is fully appropriate—as long as one's choices are reached and defended through the methods of critical values consciousness, and made in the context of an open, free, and fair discussion of the alternatives.

There is a point at which the discussion of the ultimate ends and values of life becomes inappropriate in certain types of colleges and universities, while not in others. Public institutions and those with a secular orientation should pose ultimate value questions, but not provide final answers. In contrast, institutions having a clear religious heritage will, by their very being, testify to a body of final life truths. The classroom conduct of values inquiry, however, will not necessarily be decidedly different in colleges and universities with an active religious orientation. In the first place, like any form of valuing, religious commitments have no reality unless they are genuinely made and owned by an individual. Values education and value change are processes of self-discovery. Secondly, most religious traditions would insist that a religious set of values or virtues like faith, hope, and love are not simple human possibilities. The self never fully succeeds in finding an adequate grounding for its own worth through its own analytical efforts. Faith is said to be a gift, not an accomplishment. It requires participation in a community of memory and hope, and does not emerge through private inquiry alone. There are many exceptions, of course, where religious truth is understood more dogmatically, but it would be a rare college or university that would claim that education could itself bestow religious faith. Like their counterparts at secular institutions, administrators and faculty members of denominational schools must assess the campus environment and the formal and informal norms by which their institution is governed. What is the real classroom and dormitory attitude toward religious faith—studied indifference, uncritical acceptance, or supportive questioning? What public and private occasions exist for the sharing and communication of the tradition? Are they important in the lives of faculty members and students or are they dying rituals? Religious values, like any others, need to be embodied in communal life and relationships if they are to assume their full reality.

Conclusion

Values education, as we have defined it, offers promising possibilities for higher education. It responds effectively to the educational and social concerns that stand behind the current interest in ethics, morals, and values. As well, it is able to provide adequate answers to the cautions and questions that any proposal to teach morality, ethics, or values immediately encounters in the academic world. We believe that values education offers more effective responses and more adequate answers than do related approaches like values clarification, values inquiry, moral development, or ethics. Values education—as values analysis, consciousness, criticism, pedagogy, and development—provides a wider region within which to situate the educational issues and to discuss the academic questions. It illuminates the reasons that the active interest in moral education in all its forms has arisen in the first place. It takes a broad view of the educational horizon and locates the discussion in the context of trends in liberal and professional education. It responds to the specific suspicions and issues about teaching values and ethics with more integrative answers than do other approaches. At the same time, values education does not repudiate the contributions that different methods have to offer. Rather, it seeks to integrate and synthesize many of their emphases by providing a basic perspective on human agency, values, and choice—the very issues and themes that all the approaches share.

We have already presented detailed arguments in support of the foregoing claims and need not repeat them here. Rather, we will briefly recapture many of our important conclusions and claims by considering the role of values in overcoming the fragmentation prevalent in higher education. Values education is characterized by a consistent effort to integrate what other approaches divide. We have found this integrative movement strongly at work in the drawing together of the opposites in the following antitheses:

1. Fact and Value. As standards of choice, values have a relational objectivity that make them an appropriate focus for normative inquiry, for determining what ought to be done. Facts and values are not simple opposites. They are different, yet inseparable, dimensions of all human situations. Facts always exist in some pattern of selection and valuing, and values necessarily are mediated through factual conditions.

2. Thought and Action. Values, at one level, bridge the gap between knowing and doing, by serving as the self's unifying structures of intention, choice, and enactment. To hold a value is to act on it, and to think under its authority. On the social plane, an examination of values displays the actual and potential unity of theory and practice in social, political, and moral issues.

3. Absolutism and Relativism. Based on an understanding of values as standards of choice, values education is able to overcome the stale alternatives of value absolutism and relativism. Values orient choice toward the fulfillment of human possibility, but do not function as ahistorical and unchanging absolutes.

4. Educational Form and Content. Values education emphasizes both the importance of the way values are addressed as well as the formal subject matter in which they are studied. It overcomes the common split between an exclusive emphasis either on pedagogical method or the transmission of information through academic specialties.

5. Moral Form and Content. Values education is a *process* that is able to influence moral *content*. Because values are present in all human situations, the process of values analysis, consciousness, and criticism is able to provide us with guidance in our choice among alternatives. The procedures of critical value inquiry inevitably affect the substance of value choices.

6. Curricular Specialization and Integration. Values education relies on disciplinary specialties in their proper spheres, but protects against educational fragmentation by offering liberal education an effective interdisciplinary and integrative theme.

7. Living and Learning. Values provide the point of connection between the classroom and campus life, between academic and personal experience. They offer a theme around which to construct a truly unified educational program.

8. Affect and Cognition. Thinking, feeling, and doing occur only as there is a self to which to refer them, and who takes responsibility for them. Affect and cognition are inseparable dimensions of the unified experience of the self. Values, which provide the structures and patterns for the self's identity and agency, come to expression in affect and cognition. In studying values, we study the self as a unity.

9. Intellect and Conscience. The intellect apprehends values pre-
    cisely as the norms of conscience, and not as abstract principles
    separate from human action. The self-evaluation by conscience
    is simultaneously an intellectual and affective task with a direct
    influence on conduct.

These various integrative movements reveal that the subject
of education is not simply an intellect, a mental substance, or a
complex organism, but a person who thinks, feels, and acts through
values. Only by positing this unity—the priority and oneness of
being as a person—is it possible for educators to address their
students as persons. The adequacy of the educational perspectives
that we have presented fully depends on the adequacy of our
assumptions about human experience and possibility. Other approaches can provide persuasive accounts of a number of educational goals and achievements, but ultimately are unable to
integrate knowledge and information with values and choice.

As this integrative perspective makes clear, values education
does not substitute for or replace the enormous variety of intellectual tasks and skills involved in good scholarship and effective
education. Values are not in any sense all that must be known and
studied in the human realm, although they have a central place in
experience and education. Unquestionably, the study of ideas, concepts, images, symbols, attitudes, emotions, and the like, constitute
major and continuing themes of importance. Values education
needs to be closely tied to the best efforts of scholarship in all the
fields that study human choice and conduct. Its aims should be to
add a new perspective to these investigations, to transform and not
to repudiate existing goals. To do otherwise is for it to risk becoming a poorly understood, short-lived, and even resented endeavor,
unrelated to the daily work of the academy.

Values education must avoid other errors as well; it must
neither expect nor claim too much. The powers of values education, like those of higher education, are real but limited. As we
have seen, certain depths of the human person are simply beyond
its grasp. The tasks of values education can best be carried out in
the context of a trusting and inspired realism. Through hard and
patient work, values education can crystallize higher education's

efforts into new forms and give reality to its historic promises. It can enhance the long-standing effort within liberal education to bring facts and meanings, action and reflection, social responsibility and intellectual discipline into an authentic whole. It can crystallize, too, the struggling efforts of professional studies to educate for responsibility as well as technical expertise. As the standards of human self-enactment, values offer rich and distinctive educational possibilities. Values education at its best provides a way to integrate the search for truth with the quest for integrity, and to bind the norms of intellect to the demands of conscience.

Reconciling Philosophical and Social Science Perspectives on Values

➤➤➤➤➤➤➤⫷⫷⫷⫷⫷⫷⫷

The interpretation of values offered in this work has emerged from a variety of sources. It is informed by a survey of the perspectives on values that are found in representative social science literature as well as in philosophy. The results of such a review, needless to say, are bewildering in their complexity and diversity. Nevertheless, several characteristic patterns and issues do appear across the various fields, and it is worthwhile to chart some of these here. There is a second reason to sketch these relationships. At least at one level, our position on values represents an effort to draw on insights from both the social sciences and philosophy. The dominant form of analysis that has been used, however, is a particular philosophical method that employs some of the techniques of existential phenomenology. Since methodology is always so controlling in the study of human experience, a short discussion of the assumptions of our approach also is in order.

Every field that investigates human experience addresses values in one way or another, if only tacitly. Social scientists have repeatedly explored the topic of values, often in a direct and systematic way. These studies ordinarily emphasize values as a person's or a group's internalized patterns and standards of choice and belief. The central concerns of social scientists typically are the ways in which values are acquired through socialization and how values affect particular spheres of behavior. (Much of contemporary economics is an exception to this generalization since its dominant interest is in the value of things.) When an individual internalizes a value, it becomes part of the structure of the individual's personality, or enters into the definition of his social roles. In the words of Talcott Parsons and his colleagues: "All types of cultural patterns may be internalized, but particular importance is to be attributed to the internalization of value orientations, some of which become part of the superego structure of the personality and, with corresponding frequency, of institutionalized role-expectations" (1951, p. 22).

The notion of internalization is an intriguing one. It connects values with motivation, attitude, and choice—understood as the interior psychic dynamics of human action. The term *internalization* and the process it describes, however, tend to ascribe a subjective aura to the nature of values, whether this is intended or not. The term has inclined certain theorists to equate values with these internalized preferences, to sever them from objective structures. For example, E. L. Thorndike, one of the great forebears of contemporary educational and behaviorist psychology argued that "Values, positive and negative, reside in the satisfaction felt by animals, persons or deities. If the occurrence of X can have no influence on the satisfaction or discomfort of any one present or future, X has no value, is neither good nor bad, desirable nor undesirable. Values are functions of preference" (1936, p. 2). This tendency to equate values with preferences continues to represent a common approach within psychology and other behavioral sciences. Milton Rokeach, an influential contemporary psychologist, defines a value as, "An enduring belief that a specific mode of conduct or end-state of existence is personally or socially preferable to an opposite or converse mode of conduct or end-state of existence" (1973, p. 5).

This tendency to understand values as preferences has been part of a wider effort in sociology, anthropology, political science, and economics to explain values functionally. Values are analyzed in terms of their contribution to the establishment and continuity of a social, political, or economic system. They are variously depicted as important social conventions. The theorist who may set out to offer only a functional analysis of values, however, frequently produces an exhaustive account of their very existence. Scholars have proposed biological, behaviorial, and economic principles of interpretation that explain values as wholly and simply a function of a primary organic, psychic, or social dynamic. Values have been depicted as primary components in the ideology of a ruling class, as the conditioned preferential responses of the human organism, as the constraints imposed by the superego, and as genetically determined social responses relating to the elemental value of survival. Such explanations merely explain away what they seek to understand. The important point for our purposes is that these analysts make values a function of an allegedly more fundamental reality. A given methodology circumscribes—and then completely exhausts—the reality of values.

By no means do all social scientists operate in these ways in studying values, but these tendencies dominate and color much of the work that has been done. But a human activity such as valuing is difficult, if not impossible, to grasp in its wholeness through any single empirical description. Most of the social scientists' methodologies, however, posit that the whole can be studied only when decomposed into parts or cracked into machine-readable bits. (There are, of course, many exceptions to these generalizations. In psychology, for example, see Smith, 1964.)

One would expect to find a lively interest in values among the humanities. Although this may be implicitly true, the commitment to value-free inquiry has displaced the language of values from systematic use in most contemporary fields. Among the hu-

manities, one turns, of course, to the fields of philosophy and religious studies for theoretical accounts of the nature of values. But
in neither of these fields has the nature of values been a featured
topic of many recent works in English. A number of discussions in
ethics and metaethics relate to this issue, however, and there are
signs of a growing interest. This new congeniality, together with
earlier work in field and the contributions of thinkers writing in
languages other than English, can provide a useful orientation to
the philosophy of value.

The philosophical agenda ordinarily begins with the generic
problem of the nature of value. Philosophers are concerned with
the question of how objects, ideas, and acts have value or possess
worth. Although, as we shall see, the philosophers' answers come in
different forms, they nearly always depict value as a quality. For
some theorists, value is an independent essence, while for others it
exists only in particular things. Both groups, however, generally
agree that value has specific "carriers," that value appears or is
embodied in physical objects or in states of affairs. We find value in
the justice of a law, the kindness of an act, the beauty of a painting,
and the usefulness of a tool. As a quality, value is special, and by no
means identical with the physical and other properties of things. It
has been termed a nonnatural or unreal quality.

Much philosophical discussion has surrounded the issue of
whether value is an objective or a subjective reality. The question
can be put quite simply: Are things valuable because we value
them, or do we value them because they are valuable? Or, similarly,
is value attributed to a thing because it is desired, or because it is
desirable? Theorists who hold that values are subjective tend to
equate value with the satisfaction of a felt need, or with a thing's
being an object of interest. R. B. Perry defines value thus: "A thing,
whatever it may be, has value, or is valuable, in its original or
generic sense when it is an object of interest, no matter what it (the
interest) may be. Or, that which is an object of interest is *ipso facto*
valuable" (1954, p. 3). As R. Frondizi (1963) suggests, it should be
noted that the term *interest* is being used by Perry in a rather broad
sense to refer to the complex set of actions, attitudes, dispositions,
and purposes involved in being in favor of or opposed to something. Theorists who view values as objective, on the other hand,

posit values as self-existent essences whose reality is independent of the feelings of an observer. According to Max Scheler, "The phenomenological fact is that precisely in the sentimental perception of a value there appears that very same value, as distinguished from its perception—all of which is valid in every possible case involving a sentimental perception—and consequently, the disappearance of sentimental perception does not eradicate the essence of value" (1959, p. 9). The existence of values is completely independent, thus, of the ways in which they are grasped or apprehended.

Our purpose in providing this brief sketch of objective and subjective theories is twofold. The controversy raises some of the perennial issues about the nature of value, but beyond that reveals the range of terminological problems that ensue. The terms *values* and *value* are used in significantly different ways in the social sciences and in philosophy, especially in the Anglo-American tradition. (Most of existential philosophy constitutes an exception to this generalization.) Social scientists are primarily concerned with values as standards of personal or group choice, as internalized patterns of belief and conduct. People hold or have a value as an orientation to choice, as, for example, Americans are typically said to value achievement in their orientation to success. Values, in other words, involve a way of living. In the usual philosophical discussion, on the other hand, a value is a quality, or it is a thing or act having that quality. To hold a value means to claim that a given object or action has worth, or to affirm the qualities that it possesses; holding a value does not refer primarily to a self-involving pattern or a consistent orientation to choice. In philosophy, valuing is often depicted as a discrete thought or action by means of which a person takes an interest in some external object, quality, or deed. To claim that honesty is a value, then, is to affirm honesty as an ideal, as a quality, rather than to be honest.

These very different perspectives are particularly evident in the contrasting ways in which the word *values* (as opposed to *value*) is used in the two fields. In much of traditional philosophy, the term *values* is simply the plural of *value* and refers either to a list of specific things and acts that have value, or to the qualities that are embodied in them. The plural *values* has not been used widely in philosophy to characterize the manifold dominant motivations or ways of life people adopt, as has been the case in the social sciences. In philosophy, the discussion of habits and standards of choice tends to occur much more typically under the rubric of the virtues—the excellences of choice that are appropriate to human beings as human beings. This discussion does not equate values (as standards) with virtues, but suggests that both have a similar kind of existence as immanent dispositions to choice.

These distinctions can be summarized in the following brief analysis, adapted from Najder (1975), of three common usages of the terms *value* and *values*.

1. Value is a quality or property ascribed to something (acts, things, objects) possessing that quality. Value may, for example, be attributed to compassion as a quality, as when one says, "Compassion is the greatest of the virtues." Or, it may be ascribed to certain compassionate acts, as in the claim, "It is good to care for the sick." These usages tend to be the dominant ones in most philosophical discussions of value. In subjective theories, value-qualities are mere abstractions from acts that have the appropriate characteristics. In objective theories, however, these qualities are depicted as self-existent essences or ideals, as in the traditional trio of Truth, Beauty, and Goodness.
2. Value is a belief about the desirable in terms of which objects, acts, events, institutions, and so forth, are considered to be valuable. So, for instance, we speak commonly of the values of a person or of a society as the internalized standards that determine the choices that are made. This usage is common in many of the social sciences.
3. Value is the worth of a thing. One can often measure this value in quantifiable or comparative terms. The value of a house is an example of a quantifiable economic value. (This usage does not have any special relevance to values education, thus we will not further explore it.)

Our earlier study of values clarification and values inquiry, and the present review of value theory in the social sciences and in philosophy, reveal the need for new ways to approach values. The perspectives of the social sciences and of philosophy each have important emphases that need to be considered and, in a certain sense, combined to form a theoretical framework for values education. The fundamental philosophical question of the nature of value needs to be approached again, but in close relation to the question of how values function immanently in the choices and decisions of everyday life. Philosophers tend to overlook the latter question, and social scientists the former. The distinction and relationship between the two approaches is crucial, but usually is neglected in most discussions of the place of values in higher education. As we have seen on a number of occasions, most of the methods for analyzing values tend to approach them as either emotional or cognitive objects. Without some attention to an appropriate methodology for studying values as lived, educators will maintain these inadequate fissures, and the special possibilities of values education will remain lost from view.

H. Richard Niebuhr provides helpful guidance in moving beyond the unrewarding disagreements between objective and subjective theories of value. When we face real problems among real human beings, these theories seem to make little practical difference. If we are considering the quality of justice in an actual society, we look at the existing legal, moral, and social institutions. Value becomes a matter of what is good for real human beings living in competitive and cooperative relations. Nothing seems to be gained, Niebuhr (1960) asserts, by describing these relations and the value choices they represent as "emotional preferences" or as "essences."

The foregoing point suggests that whenever value theorists turn to practical problems, they operate with *relational* models of value. Niebuhr sees as an unavoidable underlying pattern of thought in practice—regardless of theoretical intent—a relationism in which value is defined by reference to a being for which other beings are good. Relational approaches to values are not confined to the practical applications of subjectivism and objectivism. Relationalism can be expressed as a theory in its own right:"Its fundamental observation is this: That value is present where-ever one existent being with capacities and potentialities confronts another existent that limits or completes or complements it. Thus, first of all, value is present objectively for an observer in the fittingness or unfittingness of being a being" (Niebuhr, 1960, p. 103). The "being" Niebuhr refers to here is equivalent to "an existent reality." In questions of value for human beings, the "other existence" could be another person, an object, an idea, an action, and so forth. The basic notion is that of complementarity—that value is present whenever constitutive needs and possibilities are fulfilled (or at least not violated) in relation to and in terms of the given features of some other existing reality. For instance, true propositions, not errors, have worth in relation to the human mind as nutritious foods, not poisonous ones, have value with regard to, or for, the body. In each case, there is complementarity—the structural possibilities and capacities, not wants or desires, of one being are fulfilled or satisfied by another reality. There are objective characteristics on each side that make the relationship what it is.

This relational perspective suggests that value is neither an exclusively subjective or objective reality. Elements from each of these views need to be incorporated into an adequate theory. Value is understood best as arising in the relations among beings. As such, value is not simply a function of preference or desire. In the human realm, we can find knowable objective features that determine whether the constitutive needs and capacities of persons are being fulfilled or denied. We can discover whether a proposition has truth, or an action possesses moral worth, or medication restores health by examining the given characteristics of human thought, relationships, and physical well-being. Thinking a thing true or false, good or ill, surely does not make it so. At the same time, it is difficult to conceive of worth or value as independent of the potential or structure of some particular being. Value, then, is always *for* someone or something, and is not a self-sufficient reality or ideal.

These brief and basic philosophical considerations about the nature of value provide some of the background for the interpretation of values offered in this book. In turning our attention from value to values, however, we were able to address the internalization or immanence of values—which is the typical concern of the social sciences—by means of a philosophical point of departure. We depicted value as coming to reside in values as standards of human agency. We discovered the link between values and human choice and action to be profound and intimate; and, we found that values have an objective existence in terms of human meaning and possibility.

The genesis of an appropriate methodology has been a central, implicit concern throughout our interpretation of values. Any systematic study of a dimension of human experience as complex as valuing obviously depends on a method of reflection and analysis. In our era, as the modern crisis in the knowledge of man has continued to deepen, the question of method has become increasingly central. Our culture no longer shares an intellectually authoritative vision of human limits, purposes, and possibilities. The great images of human freedom and dignity that control our self-understanding, and that spawned our social and political institutions, now exist as bequeathed moral capital. We draw from them as an inheritance that we did not earn and cannot now produce on our own. Our prevailing analytical methods of thinking about ourselves provide no encompassing vision and virtually no guidance in what it means to be human. This problem, which is a deeply serious one for all educators, returns us finally to the issue of appropriate ways to study human conduct and experience.

One of the most compelling features of contemporary intellectual analysis is the use of the methods of science to study human experience. Although each discipline and subdiscipline of the natural and social sciences has its procedural or methodological distinctiveness, the sciences in concert have contributed an emergent image of humanity. They show us a humankind that is standing at the intersection of an infinite number of human and nonhuman forces and causes. According to the scientific model, we acquire knowledge of man as scientists trace qualities of human experience and modes of action to their measurable, underlying causes. In such an intellectual milieu, the study of the normative dimension of human experience becomes problematic and even impossible. As we have seen, even if scholars do not explicitly so argue, an implicit premise of most contemporary scholarship is that values and moral action are the epiphenomenal products of more basic and quantifiable forces, whether these be neural changes, chemical processes, libidinal energies, genetic patterns, positive reinforcement, or economic interests. Too often, theorists make the easy, but controlling and fatal, assumption that the analysis of one aspect of experience can explain the whole of it. Thus, a behavioral, or psychoanalytic, or genetic, or functional account of values is given as a total explanation of the human phenomenon as such. The question of how a single angle of vision, which by definition is partial, can totally explain a phenomenon is never addressed. Psychological, sociological, political, and economic accounts of values are worthy endeavors as long as no one analysis claims or assumes, either directly or inadvertently, to provide an exhaustive and comprehensive explanation of the very nature and total existence of human experience—an explanation that its own methodology prohibits it from offering. Mary Midgley (1978, pp. 5–6) provides a clear and simple illustration of the limited scope of any single description:

> What counts as a fact depends on the concepts you use, on the questions you ask. If someone buys stamps, what is going on can be described as "buying stamps," or as the pushing of a coin across a board and the receiving of paper in return—or as a set of muscular contractions—or one of stimulus-response reactions—or of a social interaction involving role playing—or a piece of dynamics, the mere movement of physical masses—or an economic exchange—or a piece of prudence typical of the buyer. None of these is *the* description. There is no neutral terminology. So there are no wholly neutral facts. All describing is classifying according to some conceptual scheme or other. We need concepts in order to pick out what matters for our present purpose from the jumble of experiences, and to relate it to the other things that matter in the world.

Clearly, then, if proponents of a given approach wish seriously to accept the ambitious task of total explanation and description, they would first have to establish their approach as both uniquely comprehensive and fundamental, and as somehow logically or factually prior to other perspectives. This proof could not include appeals to the approach's own language and methods, for that would involve circularity and arbitrariness. The justification would have to be based on criteria of validity, comprehensiveness, adequacy, and consistency that were wider than the original approach itself. Success would depend, in effect, on the establishment of a persuasive world view or a comprehensive metatheory of knowledge.

Our earlier and brief review of philosophical thinking about values provides a sense of the methods at work in this field. During the past several decades, the dominant concentration in philosophy has been on the meaning and use of the language and logic of value, rather than on the substantive nature of value and values. Those philosophers who place more credence in the possibility of the constructive powers of reason to discover metaphysical truths rely on a traditional method. They assert that human values such as freedom, truth, and justice can be discovered by the process of rational inference. Observing specific factors in human thought and life, they allege that these can be explained only by inferences about the existence of values as essences and ideals. The appearance of truth, for example, is in itself partial and incomplete and requires us to posit the existence of truth as an essence, if we are to depict reality as coherent. Thus, the existence of truth as a value can be legitimately inferred, these philosophers claim, from empirical instances of it.

The inadequacy of rational inference as a method for establishing values is acutely apparent to most modern thinkers. To infer that values exist as rational structures of intelligibility seems in no sense required. Why does the world have to have a hidden coherence? In the words of Albert Camus, "Thought, to be sure, may require that there be explanations, that the universe be coherent to our thought and responsive to our search for intelligibility. But, in fact, the universe is not at all thus intelligible—it is absurd in the precise sense that what our spirits require of it is exactly what it fails to manifest. The order that thought requires is merely a human cry flung out at a dark, unfeeling, irrational mystery which neither knows nor heeds such requirements" (in Gilkey, 1969, pp. 221–222). At most, values are fragile human inventions—bounded by the absurd.

The failure of rational inference to depict values as a fundamental form of human experience does not free us of the need to offer an alternative. Many contemporary thinkers, especially in the humanities, bemoan the circumstances we have described, but offer little in the way of an alternative, systematic approach to the problem at hand. More is needed than rhetorical warmth about human dignity. We have sought to analyze values neither as empiricists nor as rationalists, but with basic techniques derived from a phenomenological perspective. This approach is predicated on an important assumption: that we must begin with the given forms of human experience as lived. Valuing is one of many forms of human consciousness that is given with life itself. Rather than follow the mainstream of the Western philosophical tradition by first asking how we will know the good that we are to seek, the phenomenologist attempts to unveil the actual conditions under which the good becomes present in life. It is inconceivable that values—the good for humankind—could be like a king in exile, anxiously awaiting the right moment to make a triumphant appearance. Humanity cannot defer the reality and necessity of choice until a brilliant new study clarifies the nature of values. Values are already here. They are present to the extent that people communicate, choose, think, act, and feel. They are here, then, as conditions of possibility for human presence in the world.

Value relationships exist everywhere in the practically infinite interactions of individuals with their world. The human terrain of values is patterned and delimited. There could be no human world if trust and honesty, truth and order, care and respect did not have some hold on us. The phenomenologist of values wants to know what makes these given relationships possible at all. Phenomenological description is "pure" in that it is directed to the *structures* of valuing, where structures are the forms of activity, the patterns and standards of choice, that make a given experience a possibility. No inferences are required to discover values as structures, for they present themselves as constituting and making possible experience as it is. To try to remove the value is to change that given situation into some other. In this method of reflection, empirical and cultural conditions are important and highly revelatory indices of the existence of these structures, but they are not exhaustive explanations. Factual data alone, however, fail to reveal the conditions of possibility for the self's very relationship with the world. The thin-edged possibility of this relationship gains the phenomenologist's attention, though always in and through and with the factual conditions of which it is the structure. Love of neighbor necessarily occurs in a given cultural and psychological context. But this context is only a mediator of a relational actuality that makes a place for itself in the world.

The techniques of phenomenology thus offer the tools with which we can reach into the nature of lived human existence. While other approaches split experience into artificial moments, phenomenological analysis seeks to grasp it in wholeness. This method can enable us to do intellectual justice to the actual, though often tacit, moral commitments that make human existence in selfhood what it is. Phenomenological description is neither total nor exhaustive; it cannot be used to describe the important empirical differences in the psychological, social, or political ways values are implemented. Nor can we use descriptive analyses of the value structures of selfhood to urge that such structures be accepted or rejected. But phenomenological description enables us to confront the meaning of values as forms of human experience. And it enables us to show what occurs when values go unrealized—the self diminishes in its actuality and its potential, it declines in its characteristic freedom to experience the world as a dwelling place. If one wants to be a person in this world, then one cannot escape certain basic demands. These demands are values.

Annotated Bibliography of Current Literature

-»»-»»-»»-»»-»»-»»«-«-«-«-«-«-«

Many of the books and articles that have been referred to in this book deserve further study. A few words on some of the more influential or helpful sources may be useful to those readers who wish to pursue a given topic in greater depth.

Values Clarification. The first major work on values clarification was *Values and Teaching* by Louis E. Raths, Merrill Harmon, and Sidney B. Simon (1966). It contains one of the fullest discussions of the theoretical foundations of values clarification as well as several chapters on applications. *Values Clarification,* by Simon, Leland W. Howe, and Howard Kirschenbaum (1972), is perhaps the most widely available handbook, containing dozens of different classroom strategies. A somewhat more philosophical approach to values clarification, offering a broad theory of human development, is found in Brian P. Hall's *The Development of Consciousness*

(1976). Hall also has authored a series of workbooks, under the title *Value Clarification* (1973), in which he relates values clarification to various kinds of counseling programs as well as to classroom teaching. *Readings in Values Clarification,* edited by Kirschenbaum and Simon (1973), is a useful collection of essays about the applications of values clarification to teaching in a variety of fields, from religious education to mathematics. The collection also contains a discussion of related approaches and several articles that are critical of values clarification.

Values Inquiry. Earl McGrath's work provides the best illustration of the general possibilities of studying values. His monograph *Values, Liberal Education and National Destiny* (n.d.) provides the fullest account of his views and surveys two or three model programs. The Association of American College's two periodical publications, *Liberal Education* and *Forum for Liberal Education,* regularly publish articles and studies relating to the theory and practice of values education.

Moral Development. Lawrence Kohlberg and his associates have published a large number of articles and research studies on cognitive moral development. These have not been published in book form. "Stages of Moral Development as a Basis for Moral Education," one of Kohlberg's more comprehensive studies appears in *Moral Education,* edited by Beck, Crittenden, and Sullivan (1971). A very useful essay that presents the background of developmental theory is "Development as the Aim of Education," coauthored by Kohlberg and Rochelle Mayer (1971). Several critical studies of Kohlberg's position have been brought together in a comprehensive collection edited by Thomas Lickona, *Moral Development and Behavior: Theory, Research, and Social Issues* (1976). Many of the articles are written from the perspective of the behaviorist and experimental schools of psychology and provide an interesting contrast with Kohlberg's developmental assumptions.

Three studies of moral development during the college years are all worth careful examination. Perry's *Forms of Intellectual and Ethical Development in the College Years* (1970), Chickering's *Education and Identity* (1969), and Heath's *Growing Up In College* (1968) each provide an extremely useful framework for considering the moral possibilities of the total college experience and relate relatively technical discussions to the realm of practice. These three works and a number of others are helpfully summarized in a study edited by Knefelkamp, Widick, and Parker called *New Directions for Student Services: Applying New Developmental Findings* (1978). This collection also offers a useful discussion of the ways developmental theories can provide an orientation for student services.

Normative and Applied Ethics. The study by the Hastings Center of the teaching of ethics provides a comprehensive review of current trends in the teaching of ethics in higher education. The complete study includes a report which surveys developments, *The Teaching of Ethics in American Higher Education,* by Daniel Callahan and Sissela Bok (1980a). A collection of essays edited by Callahan and Bok, *The Teaching of Ethics* (1980b) presents a variety of studies on professional ethics, the history of ethics, and other topics. The Hastings Center has also published a series of monographs on ethics in the professional fields of law, medicine, business, journalism, public policy, and engineering.

The Theory of Values. One of the most thorough and interesting studies of values from the perspective of the social sciences was written some thirty years ago by Clyde Kluckhohn and appears in *Toward a General Theory of Action* by T. Parsons and others (1951). A contemporary value theorist in psychology whose work is of note is Milton Rokeach. His lengthy work *The Nature of Human Values* (1973) provides an excellent orientation to values theory and contains a number of implications for education.

Baier and Rescher's edition *Values and the Future: The Impact of Technological Change on American Values* (1971) presents an interesting interdisciplinary study of values. The editors, who are philosophers, provide a lengthy conceptual orientation to value theory as a basis for analyses of values change from the perspective of various social sciences. H. Richard Niebuhr's difficult but superb short essay "The Center of Value" is available in his *Radical Monotheism and Western Culture* (1960). Mary Midgley's engaging study *Beast and Man: The Roots of Human Nature* (1978) offers a number of important perspectives on values.

The themes of values pedagogy and development are interwoven in many of the works cited here.

References

Baier, K., and Rescher, N. (Eds.). *Values and the Future: The Impact of Technological Change on American Values.* New York: Free Press, 1971.

Bohm, D. "On Insight and Its Significance, for Science, Education and Values." *Teachers College Record,* 1979, *80,* 403–418.

Bok, D. "Can Ethics Be Taught?" *Change,* October 1976, *8,* 26–30.

Bressler, M. "The Academic Ethic and Value Consensus." *Rockefeller Foundation Working Papers: The Search for a Value Consensus.* New York: Rockefeller Foundation, 1978.

Buber, M. *Between Man and Man.* (R. G. Smith, Trans.) Boston: Beacon Press, 1955.

Callahan, D., and Bok, S. "The Role of Applied Ethics in Learning." *Change,* September 1979, *11,* 23–27.

Callahan, D., and Bok, S. *The Teaching of Ethics in American Higher Education: A Report of the Results of a Study by the Hastings Center.* Hastings-on-Hudson, N.Y.: Hastings Center, 1980a.

Callahan, D., and Bok, S. (Eds.). *The Teaching of Ethics.* New York: Plenum Press, 1980b.

Carnegie Council on Policy Studies in Higher Education. *Fair Practices in Higher Education: Rights and Responsibilities of Students and Their Colleges in a Period of Intensified Competition for Enrollments.* San Francisco: Jossey-Bass, 1979.

Carnegie Foundation for the Advancement of Teaching. *Missions of the College Curriculum: A Contemporary Review with Suggestions.* San Francisco: Jossey-Bass, 1977.

Chickering, A. *Education and Identity.* San Francisco: Jossey-Bass, 1969.

Clouser, K. D. "Medical Ethics: Some Uses, Abuses and Limitations." *Arizona Medicine,* January 1976, *33*, 44–49.

Davis, R. G. "The Mind Without Walls—or Roof." *Seminar Reports,* Columbia University, N.Y., November 14, 1973, *1*, 5.

Delattre, D. J., and Bennett, W. J. "Where the Values Movement Goes Wrong." *Change,* February 1979, *11*, 38–43.

DiGiacomo, J. J. "Ten Years as Moral Educator in a Catholic High School." In T. C. Hennessy (Ed.), *Value/Moral Education: The Schools and the Teachers.* New York: Paulist Press, 1979.

Donnellan, M., and Ebben, J. (Eds.). *Values Pedagogy in Higher Education.* Proceedings of a National Conference on Values Pedagogy in Higher Education, Siena Heights College (Adrian, Mich.), April 1978.

Eddy, E. D. *The College Influence on Student Character.* Washington, D.C.: American Council on Education, 1959.

Erikson, E. H. *Childhood and Society.* New York: Norton, 1963.

Etzioni, A. "The Importance of Humanistic Sociology." *Chronicle of Higher Education,* January 19, 1976, p. 32.

Fenton, E. (Ed.). "Cognitive-Developmental Approaches to Moral Education: Symposium." *Social Education,* 1976, *40*, 186–222.

Fingarette, H. *Self-Deception.* New York: Humanities Press, 1969.

Frederick, W. C. "Education for Social Responsibility: What the Business Schools Are Doing About It." Presentation at the annual meeting of Association of American Colleges, New Orleans, February 1977.

Freire, P. *Pedagogy of the Oppressed.* New York: Herder and Herder, 1970.

Frondizi, R. *What is Value?* Lasalle, Ill.: Open Court, 1963.

Gilkey, L. *Naming the Whirlwind.* Indianapolis, Ind.: Bobbs-Merrill, 1969.

Hall, B. P. *Value Clarification as Learning Process.* Vol. 1: *A Sourcebook.* Vol. 2: *A Guidebook of Learning Strategies.* New York: Paulist Press, 1973.

Hall, B. P. *The Development of Consciousness: A Confluent Theory of Values.* New York: Paulist Press, 1976.

Hall, R. T., and Davis, J. U. *Moral Education in Theory and Practice.* Buffalo, N.Y.: Prometheus Books, 1975.

Harrison, F. R. "The Humanistic Lessons of Solzhenitsyn and Proposition 13." *Chronicle of Higher Education,* July 29, 1978, p. 32.

Hauerwas, S. *Truthfulness and Tragedy.* South Bend, Ind.: Notre Dame Press, 1977.

Heath, D. *Growing Up in College: Liberal Education and Maturity.* San Francisco: Jossey-Bass, 1968.

Heath, D. "Prescription for Collegiate Survival: Return to Liberally Educate Today's Youth." Presentation at annual meeting of Association of American Colleges, New Orleans, February 1977.

Kirschenbaum, H., and Simon, S. B. *Readings in Values Clarification.* Minneapolis: Winston Press, 1973.

Knefelkamp, L., Widick, C., and Parker, C. A. (Eds.). *New Directions for Student Services: Applying New Developmental Findings,* no. 4. San Francisco: Jossey-Bass, 1978.

Kohlberg, L. "Education for Justice: A Modern Statement of the Platonic View." In N. F. Sizer and T. R. Sizer (Eds.), *Moral Education: Five Lectures.* Cambridge, Mass.: Harvard University Press, 1970.

Kohlberg, L. "Stages of Moral Development as a Basis for Moral Education." In C. M. Beck, B. S. Crittenden, and E. V. Sullivan (Eds.), *Moral Education.* New York: Newman Press, 1971.

Kohlberg, L. "The Cognitive-Developmental Approach to Moral Education." *Phi Delta Kappan,* 1975, *56,* 670–677.

Kohlberg, L. "Moral States and Moralization." In T. Lickona (Ed.), *Moral Development and Behavior.* New York: Holt, Rinehart and Winston, 1976.

Kohlberg, L., and Mayer, R. "Development as the Aim of Education." *Harvard Educational Review,* 1971, *42,* 449–496.

Lerner, M. *Values in Education.* Bloomington, Ind.: Phi Delta Kappa, 1976.

Lickona, T. (Ed.). *Moral Development and Behavior: Theory, Research, and Social Issues.* New York: Holt, Rinehart and Winston, 1976.

Linden, R. (Ed.). "Science, Technology and Society at Cornell University: A Guide to Courses and Curricula, 1977–78." Ithaca, N.Y.: Cornell University, 1977.

Lockwood, A. L. "The Effects of Values Clarification and Moral Development Curricula on School-Age Subjects: A Critical Review of Recent Research." *Review of Educational Research,* 1978, *48,* 325–364.

McGrath, E. J. "Careers, Values and General Education." *Liberal Education,* 1974, *60,* 1–23.

McGrath, E. J. *Values, Liberal Education and National Destiny.* Indianapolis, Ind.: Lilly Endowment, n.d.

Mehl, R. *De l'autorité des valeurs [On the Authority of Values].* Paris: Presses universitaires de France, 1957.

Middleburg, M. I. *Moral Education and Student Development During the College Years: A Selective Annotated Bibliography.* Tucson: Program in Liberal Studies, University of Arizona, 1977.

Midgley, M. *Beast and Man: The Roots of Human Nature.* Ithaca, N.Y.: Cornell University Press, 1978.

Munson, H. "Moral Thinking: Can It Be Taught?" *Psychology Today,* February 1979, *12,* 48–68, 92.

Najder, Z. *Values and Evaluations.* Oxford, England: Oxford University Press, Clarendon Press, 1975.

Neusner, J. "To Weep with Achilles." *Chronicle of Higher Education,* January 29, 1979, p. 40.

Niebuhr, H. R. "Life is Worth Living." *Intercollegian and Far Horizons,* 1939, *57,* 3–4, 22.

Niebuhr, H. R. *The Meaning of Revelation.* New York: Macmillan, 1941.

Niebuhr, H. R. *Radical Monotheism and Western Culture.* New York: Harper & Row, 1960.

Niebuhr, H. R. *The Responsible Self.* New York: Harper & Row, 1963.

Parsons, T., and others. *Toward a General Theory of Action.* Cambridge, Mass.: Harvard University Press, 1951.

Perry, R. B. *Realms of Value.* Cambridge, Mass.: Harvard University Press, 1954.

Perry, W. G., Jr. *Forms of Intellectual and Ethical Development in the College Years.* New York: Holt, Rinehart and Winston, 1970.

Price, D. E. "Public Policy and Ethics." In "The Teaching of Ethics: A Preliminary Report," *Hastings Center Report,* special supplement, 1977, 4–6.

Raths, L. E., Harmon, M., and Simon, S. B. *Values and Teaching.* Columbus, Ohio: Merrill, 1966.

Raushenbush, E. *The Student and His Studies.* Middletown, Conn.: Wesleyan University Press, 1964.

Rogers, C. R. *Freedom to Learn.* Columbus, Ohio: Merrill, 1969.

Rokeach, M. *Beliefs, Attitudes, and Values: A Theory of Organization and Change.* San Francisco: Jossey-Bass, 1968.

Rokeach, M. *The Nature of Human Values.* New York: Free Press, 1973.

Sack, J. "The Confessions of Lt. Calley." *Esquire,* November 1970, *74,* 116.

Sawhill, J. "A Question of Ethics." *Newsweek,* October 29, 1979, p. 27.

Scheler, M. *Der Formalismus in der Ethik und die materiale Wertethik* [*Formalism in Ethics and Material Values*]. Bern: Francke-Verlag, 1959.

Simon, S., Howe, L., and Kirschenbaum, H. *Values Clarification.* New York: Hart, 1972.

Simpson, E. "Moral Development Research: A Case Study of Scientific Cultural Bias." *Human Development,* 1974, *17,* 81–106.

Skinner, B. F. *Beyond Freedom and Dignity.* New York: Bantam/Vintage Books, 1972.

Sloan, D. "The Teaching of Ethics in the American Undergraduate Curriculum, 1876–1976." In D. Callahan and S. Bok (Eds.), *The Teaching of Ethics.* New York: Plenum Press, 1980.

Smith, M. B. "Personal Values in the Study of Lives." In R. W. White (Ed.), *The Study of Lives.* New York: Atherton Press, 1964.

Stewart, J. S. "Clarifying Values Clarification: A Critique." *Phi Delta Kappan,* June 1975, *56,* pp. 684–688.

"The Teaching of Ethics: A Preliminary Report." *Hastings Center Report,* special supplement, 1977.

Thorndike, E. L. "Science and Values." *Science,* 1936, *83* (2140), 2.

Trow, M. "Higher Education and Moral Development." *AAUP Bulletin,* 1976, *62,* 20–27.

Watson, J. D. *The Double Helix.* New York: Atheneum, 1968.

White, R. W. (Ed.). *The Study of Lives.* New York: Atherton Press, 1964.

Wilson, J. "The Study of 'Moral Development.'" In G. Collier, P. Tomlinson, and J. Wilson (Eds.), *Values and Moral Development in Higher Education.* New York: Halstead Press, 1974.

Wilson, J., Williams, N., and Sugarman, B. *Introduction to Moral Education.* Middlesex, England: Penguin Books, 1967.

Index